# MAKE LINKEDIN™ WORK FOR YOUR BUSINESS

The complete guide
to marketing your business,
generating leads, finding
new customers and building
your brand on LinkedIn.

## Alex Stearn

This book is dedicated
to Sonia, Tony and Ollie.

# Any Questions?

Thank you for your recent purchase of 'Make LinkedIn Work for your Business' I really hope you will enjoy the book and your business will benefit greatly.

If you have any questions about the book or about social media marketing in general, please do not hesitate to contact me by email at **alex@alexstearn.com** or on **Facebook at www.linkedin.com/in/alexstearn** and I will do my best to reply as soon as possible. I also offer regular updates, ebooks and social media tips in my newsletter at www.alexstearn.com and a group on Facebook which is all about supporting each other in our social media efforts and networking. Would love you to join us at this link http://bit.ly/yourgroup

Looking forward to connecting

# WHY THIS BOOK?

SO YOU WANT to launch a LinkedIn marketing campaign for your business or maybe you've already done so and you're just not achieving the results you expected. Perhaps that's because you've found it difficult to build a sizeable following or your audience is simply not converting into paying customers.

Every day hundreds of businesses are setting out on their social media journey excited about the opportunities and possibilities that this relatively new type of marketing may be able to offer their business. Some are getting it right, reaping huge rewards, and managing to leverage the enormous power of the Internet through social media, but the majority are struggling to make it work at all. Those who are struggling often don't really understand exactly how social media works and launch into a campaign without any plan or strategy or without even knowing exactly what they are looking to achieve. They perhaps create a LinkedIn page and ask their web developer to add a 'like' or 'follow' button to their website, invite their friends and customers to join their page, and then start posting updates. After a while they realize that whatever they are doing is having little or no positive effect on their sales and they are left with the same questions:

- How do I leverage the almighty power of the Internet and LinkedIn to make money for my business?
- How do I find the people who are interested in my products?
- How do I draw these people away from LinkedIn and onto my website or blog?
- And the ultimate question, how do I convert all these people into paying customers and actually profit from LinkedIn marketing?

These businesses either continue to go round in circles waiting for a miracle to happen, give up altogether, or continue to believe that there is a way they can make social media work for their business and start looking for a solution to solve their problem.

This is exactly what I did and this is where my social media journey began. I started to look for a solution but kept coming up with the same brick walls, the same fluffy vague information about engagement, and lots of very expensive courses. I read books and blogs but they never really seemed to solve my problem and get to the heart of the matter.

I then decided to make it my mission to demystify the hype surrounding social media marketing and discover everything I possibly could about how to make all the major social media platforms work for any business. I studied literally hundreds of campaigns to see what was working and what wasn't and completely immersed myself in social media marketing until all my questions were answered. My aim was to discover how to utilize the almighty power of LinkedIn to help any business achieve their marketing goals. I made it my mission to leave no stone unturned in terms of a marketing opportunity which could help any business generate leads and ultimately increase their sales.

After 18 months of immersing myself in this subject, I am now delighted to hand this information over to you. My goal is to help you save your time and your resources and provide you with a highly effective system to make LinkedIn work for your business. In this book I am going to share with you everything you need to know to take your business to the next level and leverage the power of LinkedIn so you can achieve the highest profits, the best customers, the best ambassadors for your business, and make money 24/7.

This book is perfect for anyone who is seriously committed to growing their business and achieving incredible results. Whether you are just starting out or already up and running and uncertain how to make LinkedIn work for your business then this book is to going to teach you exactly how to do just that. You will have absolutely everything you need to learn, prepare, plan, and implement a campaign which is going to help you generate leads and find new customers.

The fact is, LinkedIn, and social media as a whole, is a game changer, a dream come true for any business and has completely revolutionized the way business is being done today. However, it is still just a marketing tool and while on the face of it seems free, if not used correctly and effectively, it is simply just a waste of your time and resources.

In this book you will not only learn the skills and strategies of LinkedIn marketing but also everything you need to know about how social media works in marketing and how to plan, prepare, and execute your campaign including:

- What social media marketing is, why it is so good, why it is absolutely essential for any business today, and why so many businesses are getting it wrong
- The psychology behind why people make buying decisions and how you can use this knowledge to succeed in your LinkedIncampaign and other social media campaigns as well
- The importance of defining your business, your brand, and your target audience and how to do this
- How to set clear goals and objectives for your social media campaign
- How to prepare your website or blog for success, capture leads, and build a highly targeted list of subscribers
- How to plan, create, maintain, and manage your LinkedIn campaign
- Detailed information about how to set up your profile on LinkedIn
- The strategies you need to implement to attract the best prospects and build and maintain a targeted following on

LinkedIn and build lasting relationships

- The importance of content and how to easily find ideas to create content for your page
- How to convert your followers into leads, paying customers, and ambassadors and brand advocates of your business
- How to constantly measure and monitor your campaign so you can steer your campaign to achieve your goals

A great deal of love and joy has gone into writing this book. Love of the subject itself and joy at the opportunity to share with you the information and knowledge within. I have devoted 18 months to researching and writing this book, along with the others in the series, in order to uncover the truth about social media. I truly hope you will be inspired and that your business will thrive and flourish by implementing the suggested strategies.

As mentioned above there are books available on Kindle and in paperback for each of the major social media platforms including Facebook, Twitter, Instagram, Google + YouTube, Pinterest and Tumblr. The big book, 'Make Social Media Work for your Business' covers includes all
8 books. If you are planning on buying more than a few books then I would suggest purchasing this book rather than each individual book. The big book 'Make Social Media Work for your Business' is available from $9.99 at this Link

Even within the time it has taken to write this book, certain things have changed in the social media world and so some sections have been updated to reflect those changes. The world of social media is dynamic and therefore it is my commitment to keep updating this book as those changes occur. If you wish to keep up-to-date with latest social media updates, tips, and changes, please subscribe to my newsletter at www.alexstearn.com

# The Social Media Master Plan & Workbook

The Social Media Planner and Workbook compliments this book and all the books in the series 'Make Social Media Work for your Business'. Once you have read the book I highly recommend that you complete this short workbook. It's designed to take you step by step through what you need to do to find your ideal customers, build your audience on social media and actually succeed to selling your products and services. It is not a substitute for reading the book but will help you apply your knowledge to your particular product or service. You can download your **Free** Ebook here:

## www.bit.ly/winsocial

# CHAPTER ONE

## *THE IMPORTANCE OF UNDERSTANDING SOCIAL MEDIA MARKETING*

BEFORE LAUNCHING INTO your LinkedIn marketing campaign, and so that you are absolutely committed when you do start, you will need to be convinced that social media marketing does actually work for businesses and that you are going to be able to make it work for yours. In this chapter, you will learn why social media marketing has gained so much attention, why so many brands are using it, and why it is so different from other forms of marketing. The aim here is to help you truly appreciate the power and importance of this relatively new method of marketing. Once you are totally convinced that the time you will be investing will be truly worthwhile, you will be ready to launch into your LinkedIn marketing campaign with strength, confidence, and conviction.

So what is social media exactly? Social media is the place where people connect with other people using the technology we have today. It's where people engage, share, cooperate, interact, learn, enjoy, and build relationships. The number of ways in which we connect with each other has grown massively in recent years from telephone, mobiles, email, text, video, newspaper, or radio to what we have today, the social media networks.

As humans, the majority of us want to belong, be accepted, loved, respected, and heard. We are social animals and social media has provided us with new tools which allow us to be more social, even if our lives are more hectic and we are living a long way from our friends and family. It's now not unusual for family and friends to be located at opposite sides of the country or even in a different country. Our lives have become far busier and more transient than ever, and yet we still crave the same social connections as we did 100 years ago when we would probably have been living in the same village or town as our family and friends.

The impact that social media is having on our lives and on businesses is massive. Social media has completely changed the way we communicate and the way we do everything. It has made connecting with people and building relationships so much easier. Now, staying in contact with someone we may only have met once is straightforward. We can find old friends we went to school or college with, and the opportunities for making new contacts are limitless. Social media has given us the ability to quickly and easily share ideas, experiences, and information on anything we like, and we can find out about anyone, any business, or anything. With the massive growth in smartphone ownership, most people can now access the internet instantly. We are living in a virtual world and we can literally connect to anyone, from anywhere, at anytime.

Understanding the reasons why people love social media so much will help give you a really good idea about how, as a business, you need to engage so you can connect,grow and maintain that your audience. Most people are on social media to be social, to connect with other family and friends, and to have fun. However, here are a few more reasons why so many use and love social media:

To be part of a community or common interest group
To express their feelings and have a voice
To reconnect with old college or school friends
To find out where their friends are
To tell their friends where they are
To announce a piece of news
To find out if a product or service is good

To connect with thought leaders

To make business contacts

To follow brands

To keep up-to-date with current affairs, football scores etc

To connect with famous people

To find inspiration and motivation

To learn by reading blogs, watching videos, and listening to podcasts

To help other people

To launch a business

To advertise and grow a business

To make new friends

To make new contacts

To connect with others in different countries

To make a difference

To be entertained

To communicate quickly and save time

To support important causes or people

To find a job

## The power and enormity of social media

Everyone is doing Social! Okay, so not everyone is, but the majority of people are! Wherever you go you will see somebody with their heads down looking at some device, and you can bet your bottom dollar that they are accessing some social site, whether it's LinkedIn, Twitter, Instagram, LinkedIn, YouTube, Google+, Pinterest, or Snapchat.

The growth in social media is huge, and it's no wonder that it is being called 'The Social Media Revolution.' Without going into too much statistical information, it's safe to say that your customer is probably using at least one social network, either for personal or business use, and they very likely accessing multiple sites.

All the social media platforms are growing at incredible speeds. You only have to type 'Social media statistics' into Google and you will blown away by figures in the millions and billions. Facebook now has over one billion users and 95% of those users access it at least once a day and some more than five times, a day More than one billion unique users visit YouTube per month, and Twitter has 215 monthly active users. The most popular websites are social. The world loves being on social.

## WHAT IS SOCIAL MEDIA MARKETING

Not long ago promoting a business could feel very much like being alone on a desert island. You could have a great idea but unless you had vast sums of money for television, magazine, or direct mail advertising then, frustratingly, your idea was very likely to remain a secret. Today it is totally different and social media has given businesses endless opportunities to reach their target audience, connect with new prospects, and enter new markets. The playing field has been levelled out, and now anyone with the right knowledge has more chance than ever of making their business a success.

Social media marketing is a relatively new form of marketing and refers to the processes, strategies, and tactics used by businesses on social networking sites and blogs to gain attention and ultimately increase their revenue. Businesses and large brands are now using the fact that people love to engage and connect with other people with the other important fact that they are very likely to find their target audience on social media so that they can do the following:

- Find, reach, and connect with potential customers
- Drive traffic to a website or blog
- Stay connected and communicate with existing customers. It is a well-known fact that existing customers are far more likely to purchase and also pay more for a product than someone who has not bought before.
- To build trust, interest, and loyalty by interacting with your followers (potential customers) so that ultimately they will purchase your product, continue to purchase your product, and hopefully recommend your product to their friends

- To produce content that users will share with their social network or recommend to their friends. Social media marketing strongly centers around the creation of content for a particular audience with the intention that it can be shared, 'liked', and commented on by the user. When this happens, the content is being passed to other users by word-of-mouth, the most powerful form of advertising.
- To listen and find out what your customers want.

## THE BIG LINK, THE PSYCHOLOGY BEHIND BUYING BEHAVIOUR

Not only have successful marketeers recognized that people want to engage with people, they have also tapped into the psychology behind why people make buying decisions and incorporated this into their social media campaigns.

As a business you will need to understand a great deal about your customers in order to market your products successfully to your target audience. Understanding how and why people make the final purchase decision will go a long way to help you discern how to make social media marketing actually work for your business. There seem to be a number of common factors that influence consumers when they are making their buying decision. Leveraging and using this knowledge with your LinkedIn campaign will be incredibly powerful and a recipe for success.

**The 'like' factor**

This is a biggie. When we look at the findings and the psychology behind buying decisions it often comes down to simply being likeable. Consumers are far more likely to buy a product from someone they like, respect, or trust. Word-of-mouth advertising has always proven to be the most powerful form of advertising and now LinkedIn has taken this to another level and managed to harness this online with the 'like' button. Having your business name or brand reach hundreds or even thousands of people is now possible, and someone only has to 'like' or interact with your business on social media and you can almost guarantee that someone else will see that interaction. The truth is people do business with people they like and are more inclined to spread the word to their network about deals and special offers from people they trust, and respect.

## Social proof

When a consumer finds themselves at a point of indecision they will look for social proof and seek advice and corroboration from others. They are far more likely to buy if they see that their friends or a similar group of people have bought or used the product. People generally seek advice or look to see what others are buying to get over their personal insecurity when making a buying decision. This is why you see so many women shopping in pairs. The opinion of a friend about an item can often be the deciding factor when making the decision to buy or not.

## Authority and reviews

Even before the Internet was introduced, people were keen to find reviews about products they were interested in buying, particularly if they were planning to make a major purchase. They would either buy a special magazine or seek information from an authoritative figure on a TV advertisement. Today, however, shoppers are far more savvy. They can smell an ad a mile off and they will go out of their way to find honest reviews about something they may want to buy. They are also spoiled for choice, not only with the number of products available to them but the fact that they can find a review about literally anything just by a simple search on the Internet or looking at a brand's social media profile. People always have and always will want as much evidence as possible that they are making the right buying decision. Any business who wants to succeed today needs to embrace this fact and try and gain as many reviews for their products and services as possible. Reviews could be in the form of customer blog articles, reviews on your website, on social media sites, or articles in newspapers and magazines. Displaying articles, client testimonials, or the logos of magazines that you have been featured in on your website will also go a long way to building authority and gaining the trust of your prospects.

## Scarcity or exclusivity

Scarcity or exclusivity can play a big part in people's buying decisions, and LinkedIn is a perfect place to communicate and use this factor to sell your products. If a product is scarce or less available, the consumer will often perceive that this product has greater value. As it becomes less available, the consumer fears that they may lose out on a great deal or a one-time offer. Giving your prospects a deadline or a specific time to purchase something or redeem an offer is an incredibly powerful way of focusing their mind on making a decision. When they know they need to make that decision by a certain time or they may lose out on a one-time deal, they are far more likely to make that decision. Another very effective way of using this factor is by simply suggesting to your prospects that by signing up for your email opt-in, they will be the first to hear about your new products or your exclusive offers.

## Loyalty

Consumers do not like taking risks and often prefer to repeat their past purchasing behavior by buying from a brand they have bought from before. The majority of shoppers are brand loyal and social media is another way of nurturing this type of behavior by building up even deeper relationships with your customers through constant contact and updates.

## Reciprocation

Reciprocation is a very powerful factor to take into consideration if you are looking to succeed on LinkedIn. As humans, the majority of us have a natural desire to repay favors and with LinkedIn you can really put this into practice. By 'liking', sharing, or commenting on other people's content, you will attract their attention.. More often than not, they will return the favor by 'liking', commenting, and sharing your content. Also, if you are sharing great content on your network or offering good, valuable, and free advice, you are very likely to earn a great deal of respect. This will often result in a good payback of some sort later.

# WHY IS SOCIAL MEDIA MARKETING SO GOOD FOR YOUR BUSINESS?

We know that an enormous number of people are accessing the social networks to connect with each other, and now we need to understand why this type of marketing is so different from other forms of marketing and why it is so important for your business. The main reason is that social media marketing is fundamentally more effective. Consumers today are smart. They are tired and suspicious of traditional forms of advertising. More often than not they will fast forward a TV commercial, switch channels, or skip a printed page with an advertisement on it. Today's consumers want to hear that a product has been tried and tested. They want to see a product being demonstrated, and they often need a recommendation from a trusted source, most likely a fried, to make a purchase. Here are some reasons why social media marketing is more effective than other, more traditional, marketing methods:

**Social media offers you the opportunity to find the right target audience.**
Never before has it been so easy to find and access your target audience. With the information that Facebook and most of the social networks hold about their users, you can now target and find the very people who are more likely to buy your products or services.

**Social media allows you to have direct contact with your customer.**
You literally have the opportunity to communicate directly and stay in touch with your customer, unlike traditional forms of advertising. For instance with a Facebook business page or a 'places' page, you can stay in touch with your customers well after they have left your establishment or bought your product. You can also send them offers to encourage them

to return or buy your product again.

## Social media marketing harnesses the power of peer recommendation.

The majority of people trust recommendations by others. Social media marketing is the only media that can harness the most powerful form of advertising, word of mouth, by making it possible for consumers to communicate with each other and vote for products or services by pressing the 'like' or 'follow' button.

## Social media helps builds your brand.

Never has there been so much opportunity to build your brand. Your brand is simply the most valuable asset of your business. Your brand is what differentiates you from other businesses. It is the image people have of your business, and it establishes loyalty. With social media you have the opportunity to engage with consumers and build positive brand associations in a way that no other media can. Consumers now have the choice and opportunity to follow your brand. If they do, this means they actually want to hear or see what you have to say.

## Social media humanizes your brand.

Social media allows you to communicate with your audience in a totally unique way. Your brand is no longer a rigid logo but a personality. Not only can you show your appreciation and the value you place on your audience, but they can also grow to love your brand too. No other type of marketing allows this type of two-way live communication.

## Offers continual exposure to your product.

Social media marketing allows you to be continually in contact with your followers. Once you build your audience, they can hear from you and see your brand on a daily basis. Statistics prove that, on average, a person needs to see or connect with a brand seven times before purchasing. This is a difficult and costly goal to achieve with traditional forms of advertising but incredibly easy with social media marketing.

### The consumer has a choice.

Unlike other traditional methods of advertising, the consumer has the opportunity to be exposed to your product by choice. They can opt in or out whenever they want.

### Your audience is relaxed and receptive.

The majority of people are accessing Facebook and other social media accounts in their own leisure time to be social. Social media is all about connecting with friends and relatives, meeting new people and making new contacts. People are far more receptive to hearing from a brand in their own time when they are relaxed, as long as the brand is offering some kind of value and is not continually pushing their product.

### You can continually engage with your audience.

Social media marketing allows businesses to have an ongoing dialogue with their audience like no other media. Fans or followers who have interacted with a business on social media are far more likely to visit their online store than those who did not.

### It's viral.

Once your followers choose to interact or share your content then this interaction is seen by their network of friends who are then also exposed to your brand. This is how viral growth happens, which results in audience growth and brand awareness, more prospects, more customers, and increased sales.

### Social media is an asset to your business.

Unlike other forms of advertising where you see your marketing investment disappear, your Facebook page, or any other social media account, becomes a valuable asset. If you are using your social media marketing correctly, your network will grow, you will be building trust, and your asset will increase in value. With traditional advertising, once an advert is delivered the connection with the buyer is over and you see your investment literally disappear.

## It is like having your own broadcasting channel.

Once you have your campaign set up and your follower numbers are growing, you literally have your very own broadcasting channel which you own. You can communicate with your followers about anything 24/7. Nobody can take this away unless, of course, you are not running it correctly and you are losing followers. If you provide content that is so useful and interesting, your followers will keep coming back again and again to check if you have anything new to say. You then have a following of people who will associate your valuable content and their positive experience with your brand.

## You can offer your customers proof of trading.

Having a social media presence that is active and engaging helps reassure customers that your business actually exists. They can easily check, by comments left by customers, whether your business is reputable and trustworthy. They are far more likely to buy from you once they see your active presence on social media.

## Social media improves your search engine ranking.

Google counts social sharing when ranking your website or blog. If people are finding your content valuable then the search engines will register this and rank your site accordingly. Social media sites are highly ranked in the search engines and having a well-optimized profile is yet another way of being found on the Internet.

## Social media opens up a worldwide playing field.

It used to be only the large companies who could afford to build their brand and have the opportunity to access thousands of potential customers. Now everybody with a business has the opportunity to reach thousands of people, both nationally and globally, grow their business, and benefit from one of the most powerful forms of marketing. Having a business no longer needs be a lonely island. You literally have the opportunity to get your message heard by thousands of people through social networking.

**Social media provides advantages for the consumer.**

With just a few clicks of the mouse or the tap of a smartphone, consumers can be in contact with any business very quickly. For the first time they have a very powerful voice. Their opinions are taken seriously. They are and valued whether they are in contact through customer service or just following a brand because they are interested. People want to remain close to the brands they are interested in, and this is shown by the continual rise in the number of people following brands.

**You can listen to your customers.**

You can now hear what your customers are saying about your product or service, and you can use this information to improve or develop your products and customer service. This helps your business become more transparent and shows your customers that you care and value their opinion, which ultimately leads to more trust for your brand.

**You can become a thought leader.**

By producing valuable and rich content for your audience, you can become a thought leader. Not only will this help if you are a personal brand, but it will also help build trust and reputation for any business or brand.

**You can make a difference.**

With social media you can actually make a positive difference in people's lives. Once you know your audience, you can provide content which is of value to them and will actually help them in some way. Helping your audience like this goes a long way in helping them remember your business when they are ready to make that purchasing decision.

**It promotes endless opportunities.**

Never has there been so much opportunity to have direct access to so many people, and neither has there been so much opportunity for any business of any size to have ongoing contact with so many of their potential customers. This is a marketeer or business owner's dream.

## IS SOCIAL MEDIA ACTUALLY WORKING FOR BUSINESS?

It is evident that the majority of major brands are running successful social media marketing campaigns. These brands are investing huge amounts of money, time, and resources into this type of marketing. However, you don't have to go too far to see whether social media marketing is actually working for business. Simply ask yourself these questions:

• Would you prefer to buy a product if you knew that a friend or somebody you know had tried it?
• Would you prefer to buy a product from a business or person that you do know rather than a one you don't know?
• If you were thinking of buying a product from a business you had no history with, would you go and look to see if they had a social media site and find out what other people were saying about their product?

If you answered yes to these questions then you can be pretty sure that social media marketing does actually work for businesses. It has to, doesn't it?

## WHY SO MANY BUSINESSES ARE GETTING IT WRONG

Even though most business owners have heard how powerful social media marketing can be, the majority are still unsure as to how to use it to benefit their business. So many social media profiles have been created with enthusiasm only to be abandoned a couple of months, even weeks, down the line. Others are painstakingly posting consistently every day but posting the wrong type of content without a clue how to get their fans to buy their products. Many businesses are just paying lip service and seem to think that displaying a few social media icons on their site is enough to miraculously increase their revenue, and some are not even connected to any networks at all. Although on the face of it social media marketing seems free, it actually takes a sizeable investment of man hours, and if you are getting it wrong, you may as well be throwing a great deal of money out of the window. Here are some common reasons why so many businesses are getting it wrong:

## Not 100% committed and convinced

Many businesses are not convinced that it actually works at all and therefore are not prepared to put in the time it to learn how to plan and implement the effective strategies it takes to build a successful campaign. As a result, their campaign falls flat and they simply give up after a few months.

## Little or no understanding about how social media marketing works

Many still think that setting up a profile and putting an icon on their website is what it's all about. They may even post a few status updates and some pictures of their product in the hope that their website is suddenly going to be inundated with new traffic and that these new visitors are miraculously going to convert into customers.

## They don't understand the fact that fans and followers are worthless unless they know what to do with them

Just because a business has maybe 1000 or 30,000 fans or followers, it does not mean this will automatically transfer to their balance sheet. Fans are just fans, and as long a business doesn't know what do with those fans, they will stay as fans and not customers.

## Not understanding the psychology behind buying decisions

They have absolutely no idea about the psychology behind how and why people make buying decisions and, therefore, do not know how to use this knowledge to their advantage in their campaign.

## Lack of clear goals

Aimlessly sharing content on their network without setting specific and measurable goals is just a waste of time and resources.

## Not having a system to capture and convert leads

Building a following is almost useless if those followers are not visiting the business' website or subscribing to the newsletter so that they can be converted into paying customers. Many businesses are still not making lead capture one of their main goals.

## Unrealistic expectations

Social media is a long-term strategy. It needs to be an integral part of a business' marketing plan, and today, it's as important as any other daily task a business may undertake. It is not a one-size-fits-all solution nor a solution for overnight success. It takes careful planning and long-term commitment.

## The wrong audience

It's no good having a huge number of fans if they are not interested in buying your product. There are even sites where you can buy fans, but if they are not the right audience, they are very unlikely to be interested in what that business has to offer.

## Not enough followers

The majority of businesses are going to need a sizeable audience to make any impact at all. Although engagement is important, unless a business has a healthy number of followers, it's not going to be a great deal of benefit.

## Not being proactive

Many businesses seem to assume that people are just going to press the 'like' or 'follow' button on their blog or website. Unfortunately it doesn't work like that and people generally need a good reason or incentive to follow a business, unless it's a very well-known brand.

## Trying to push their products all the time

This is not what social media marketing is about. Businesses that continually push their products are just missing the whole point of how social media marketing works and will lose followers as a result.

## Posting too little, posting too often, or posting the wrong content altogether

If you post too much, your posts will be considered spam. If you post too little, you will just be forgotten. If you post the wrong content, you will not attract the right audience which may harm your brand. The top three reasons for losing fans are:

i.) The company posts too frequently

ii.) The business pushes their products too much

iii.) The business posts offensive content

## Chapter Two

## How to Run a Successful LinkedIn Marketing Campaign, an Overview

ONCE YOU HAVE made the decision to be 100% committed to your campaign, you fully understand the theory behind it, and you plan and implement the strategies and tactics outlined in this book your business is going to reap the benefits and you will in time develop an extremely valuable asset. One thing is for certain: if you choose to ignore social media, you can be sure that your competition will not and you'll be allowing them to steal the advantage. Social media is a powerful way to increase your revenue by driving sales, increasing customer loyalty, and building your brand while at the same time pushing down your cost of sales, marketing, customer service, and much more. Now let's get started!

So how do you leverage the power of social media and put it to work to benefit your business and produce amazing results? This chapter is designed to give you a brief overview about what is required to build a successful campaign so that as you read each chapter it will make more sense. Every aspect of this overview and everything you need to do and implement will be mapped out in more detail in the subsequent chapters.

The opportunity to reach an unlimited number of new contacts and prospects is available to every business today. You can safely say that your prospects are out there and all you need to do is know where to find them, how to connect with them, and how to capture and convert them into your customers.

Successful businesses are using LinkedIn and the other social media platforms in a totally different way from traditional methods of marketing. With LinkedIn marketing there is no need to employ pushy sales techniques. Once you put the essential work, planning, and system in place, you will find your products are practically selling themselves and your prospects are buying your products and becoming your brand advocates as a natural progression from your initial contact with them. The whole process is straightforward and as long as you carry out the necessary background work, planning, and preparation, you can make it work for your business.

## Know what you want

You need to have a very good idea where you want your business to be in the next one to three years. If you don't know what you want, then it is unlikely that your business will achieve anywhere near its potential. When you have a clear vision for your business, it helps you to focus and create the necessary goals you need to put into place to achieve that vision.

## Define your business, brand, and target audience

Brands establish customer loyalty, and LinkedIn offers you a huge opportunity to build your brand. In order to communicate in the right way, you need to create and consistently deliver the right message and brand experience to your prospects and customers. To do this, you need to define your business and define and understand your target audience so you can create your brand.

## Plan, plan, plan

Social media is not a quick fix. The majority of businesses start a campaign and then fall by the wayside. If you want to grow your business, then careful planning is required and it will involve creating your mission statement, setting clear and measurable goals and objectives, and planning your content strategy in line with who and what your target audience wants. Without a carefully crafted plan your campaign is extremely unlikely to reach its full potential.

## Prepare your business

Before launching your campaign you need to prepare your whole business so your brand and your brand message are evident throughout. You will need to communicate your brand through everything your do or say, including all your marketing material, brochures, promotional material, your website, your blog, and your email.

Your website is one of the best sales people you can have. It works 24/7 and can help to make your business turn up in your customer's home at the click of a mouse. When your prospect arrives on your website it immediately needs to make them feel that they have arrived at the right place, that you understand their needs, and that you can either provide a solution or give them exactly what they want. If you already have a website, you need to check that it has all the necessary features it takes to grab your visitors' attention, deliver the right message, capture them, and convert them into customers. Statistics prove that unless a business has a clever method of capturing leads, the majority of visitors to a website will leave without buying anything or ever returning again. Therefore, before even starting your LinkedIn campaign, you will need to check or create your website so that it does the job it is supposed to, which is to capture leads for later sales conversion.

## Set up your email campaign

Email is still one of the most effective methods of converting leads, and an up-to-date list of prospects who have given their permission for you to contact them on a regular basis has got to be one of your business' most valuable assets. Capturing email addresses on your website and through social media needs to be your most important marketing goal. Therefore, you will need to plan your opt-in campaign and set up an account with an email provider so you can continue to build a relationship with your prospects and sell your products.

## Create your personal profile and your company page

Your LinkedIn profile will in many cases be the first impression your prospects have about you and your business and is as important as your website or blog. The aim of your profile and your company page is to capture your prospects so that you can continue to communicate and build a relationship with them through their newsfeed.

## Create your LinkedIn posting calendar

Social media is not like traditional forms of advertising, so frequently pushing your products, posting ads, and plugging your business is not going to work and is likely to lose you fans. One of the most important things you are going to have to do for a successful LinkedIn campaign is to regularly produce and post compelling content that your audience actually wants to engage with and share. LinkedIn marketing is all about selling without selling, and the aim of producing content is not to directly sell your products but to do the following:

- Boost traffic to your blog or website, generate, capture, and nurture leads
- Create brand awareness
- Constantly remind your audience of your brand so when they are ready to buy, they buy from you
- Improve your ranking in the search engines
- Create engagement, build relationships, and encourage your audience to share your content with their friends
- Support others by 'liking', commenting on, and sharing their content
- Stand out as a thought leader and build your reputation as an expert in your industry

Create such good content that your audience stays 'liking' your page and continuing to read your updates, which builds and encourages brand loyalty.

Your content is where you can connect with your audience through their interests and passions. Your quality of content needs to be outstanding and you need to delight your audience with the best possible fresh, new, and compelling material. Excellence is what you should be aiming for with every update you make. The biggest thing to remember is that you need to tailor all your content to your audience's desires and needs.

Once you are absolutely clear about who your target audience is, what makes them tick, and what their values and aspirations are, you can determine what subjects and topics they will be interested in. The majority of the content you post will need to be about their needs and not yours. There is nothing more off putting and likely to lose you followers than continually posting about your business and shouting about your products or services. Of course you can do this occasionally if you have a new product or a special offer, but you need to be selective. Otherwise, your posts just become bad noise. Remember your followers are mostly on social media to be social. If your posts ruin their social experience, they will associate your brand with a bad experience and it won't be long before you start losing your fans and potential customers.

When you have decided on the subjects and topics you are going to create content about, you will need to create a LinkedIn posting calendar which will help you to consistently deliver this high-quality content. You will need to incorporate everything in this calendar, including any events you are planning, any special industry events, public holidays, blog posts, videos, and offers or contests you may be planning. You then need to map it all out so you know exactly how you are going to promote them on LinkedIn with the functionality you have available to do so.

## Build a sizeable and highly targeted following
The main aim of building your audience is to grow a community of followers who are interested in your products, will engage with your content, and become advocates for your brand. In order to have any impact at all you are going to need a sizeable number of targeted fans on LinkedIn. Building your audience will be an ongoing task, and it involves many different strategies which will be covered in this book. The size of audience and time it takes will depend on the time and resources you

have available.

## The essential day-to-day activity

To build a strong presence, trust, relationships, and reputation, you will need to be active and nurture your fans. Social media is not a one-way street. It's an ongoing two-way communication. It's about going out and showing that you are interested in what others have to say, and it's about building community and getting your brand out there in the most positive light possible. Here are some of the things you will need to do on a day-to-day basis:

- Consistently post high-quality content
- Follow your followers and fans
- Engage, comment, share, and reply
- Show your audience you value and respect them
- Follow influencers in your niche
- Deal with negative comments

## Analyzing and measuring your campaign results

This book is all about how to make LinkedIn work for your business, and the only way you are going to find out if it is working or not is by constantly monitoring and analyzing your results. You will need to constantly check your results against the goals and objectives you have set. Once you know what is working and what is not then you can adjust and steer your campaign accordingly to achieve more positive results.

## CHAPTER THREE

### *GETTING STARTED ON LINKEDIN*

WITH OVER 200 million members in 200 countries and an average member income of over $100,000 LinkedIn is now the worlds largest and fastest growing professional networks with it's main objective being to connect business people.

The immediate thought that usually comes to mind when thinking about LinkedIn is for recruitment and job search however it has proven to be much more. LinkedIn is not only where senior executives are headhunted and serious job seekers hang out, it is also where a great deal of business takes place. Research shows that a whopping 80% of members influence buying decisions in their companies and also members have more trust in business information they receive on LinkedIn than on any other social networks. More and more businesses are joining and seeing the additional benefits LinkedIn has to offer for building their business. Here are some of the main benefits:

**Business development & networking**
No other network offers such a high number and high calibre of business people on the internet. The opportunities to network and make new contacts are endless. LinkedIn's advanced search function allows you to search for people based on a variety of criteria which allows you to reach out to specific industry professionals including customers, suppliers and employees.

**A powerful lead generation tool**
Because of its huge business membership LinkedIn is a very powerful

source and generator of leads for any business and LinkedIn can be used to find and connect with potential customers. There are many areas that you can use LinkedIn to generate leads as follows:

- Building your personal connections
- Participating in LinkedIn Groups
- Creating your own LinkedIn group
- Creating a Company Page on LinkedIn
- Using Linkedin's powerful search for sourcing leads and contacting new prospects

**Increases your business' exposure with a company page**

LinkedIn offers you the opportunity to create a page for your company where you can upload detailed descriptions of your products and services for free which helps to increase brand's exposure amongst a network of professional people. Having a company page is like having another website except with a ready made audience that is linked to your business profile and potentially exposed to an unlimited audience of business professionals.

**Increases credibility**

Linked in offers a great opportunity to receive recommendations for your business from clients, business partners and suppliers which can be viewed on your page. This is a powerful way of building credibility and social proof with potential connections.

**Website Traffic**

LinkedIn is responsible for driving a higher proportion of social traffic to corporate websites compared to any other social networks.

**Content Sharing**

LinkedIn offers you the opportunity to share your content, your news and developments in your industry.

**Group Participation**

With LinkedIn you can participate in groups which are centred around specific topics in your niche. By joining and participating you can share your expertise with other members, comment on topics and join in conversations. All of these actions can help to build relationships with potential customers, key influencers and help to build your brand.

## Group Creation
Creating, promoting and maintaining your own group on LinkedIn will increase your exposure, influence and credibility within your niche and is great way to connect with customers and potential customers. Creating a group which is active and full of discussions and great content can help you to stand out as a thought leader, help to build your brand and gives you credibility for bringing like minded people together.

## Industry news
**LinkedInToday** helps you stay on top of whats going on in your industry and offers you the most popular articles that are being shared on your network. You can have these updates sent to your email. Being in the know and up to date with the latest trends and news assists you in your own content creation which you can also share on other networks too.

## Recruitment & Job Search
LinkedIn in offers both recruiters and job seekers some of the best information for searching for people, together with regular job news and updates.

## Google favorites
LinkedIn profiles and company pages are very well ranked in Google search.

## Builds personal brands
LinkedIn is excellent for building a personal brand based on your professional and educational background. It allows members to view your experience and qualifications and helps build trust through

credibility and history. No other network offers this amount of information about a person's education and work experience.

## It's all business

LinkedIn stands out from all the other social platforms because it's all about business. People are on LinkedIn are in a business mindset and ready to discuss and do business.

# CREATING YOUR PERSONAL PROFILE ON LINKEDIN

You need to think of your LinkedIn profile as your own professional website, there to promote your skills, knowledge, personality and your own personal brand. LinkedIn profiles are generally ranked in first or second page for your name in Google and as with every other social media network your profile needs to be fully optimised for LinkedIn search and for Google search.

To register for your account you will need to input some basic information including your name and address and your most recent position with dates. LinkedIn will then offer you the opportunity to find your current email contacts that are already LinkedIn members. It is best to leave this until your profile is fully completed and optimised.

At the next step LinkedIn will send you an email to verify your account. You can then choose if you want a basic account (free) or a premium (paid) profile. A free account is sufficient to start with and allows you to take advantage of the many benefits and opportunities that LinkedIn offers to their members. You can upgrade your membership at any time if you require any of the additional features a paid account has to offer.

## Optimising your profile for success

Once you have completed the initial sign up process you will need to complete all the sections to optimise your profile. It's worth putting a great deal of time and thought into creating an interesting, personable and authentic profile. LinkedIn is all about your professional self and lets you really go to town selling yourself with the profile features it offers. Simply click on '**Profile**' and then '**Edit Profile**' and you can add your photo, summary, work experience details and skills and expertise.

When it comes to uploading your profile picture, make sure the image you have is a high quality one and represents you in the most friendly and professional way possible.

When it comes to optimising your LinkedIn profile it's really important to complete every section in detail. The more complete your profile the higher you will appear in LinkedIn search. Here are some tips on completing the various sections on your personal profile:

**Your professional headline**

Your professional headline is found below your name on your personal profile, it is shown when you ask another member to connect with you. The headline is automatically populated by LinkedIn with your job title but you have the opportunity here to be really ahead the competition by being specific about what you offer and the value you can bring to your customers. You have 110 characters to entice your audience by writing something creative and compelling. Remember your headline is your first opportunity on LinkedIn to break the ice and start a relationship with anyone who is viewing your profile so you need to use this headline to reach out to them and grab their attention. So many individuals miss out on this marketing opportunity by not making it obvious how they can be of assistance and of benefit to their potential customers. Sometimes adding a little humor can work and not only gains attention but also helps people to remember you.

Be sure to include powerful keywords from your niche as it will affect how you are shown in Google and LinkedIn search results. You may even want to mention your business name or what country, area or region you are in, especially if your business is of a more local nature. If you are stuck for inspiration the best thing to do is check out other profiles and headlines.

## Custom profile background/Cover photo

Premium members can now upload a custom profile background. This in itself is a huge motivation to sign up as a premium member on LinkedIn and an excellent way to stand out on LinkedIn and promote your brand. You can either choose from LinkedIn's gallery of images or upload your own, the cover photo area is 1400X425 pixels.

## Personal Summary

Your personal summary is an extension of your professional headline and is a great white space to tell your story preferably in the first person. You have 2000 characters to communicate your personality, expertise and the value you can provide. The best summaries that stand out are usually inventive, authentic and interesting. You need to tell your audience who you are, what you do and how you can help them. This is also a great place to provide information about your interests beyond business, as it makes your profile more interesting, unique, memorable and personal to you. You can add videos, SlideShare presentations and other files to your summary which really help to showcase your work. You can also add a video which is particularly good if you are a personal brand, after all there is no better way of breaking the ice and helping people get to know you than by creating and including a short introduction video.

When it comes to writing make sure your paragraphs is short and snappy, in order to keep your audience interested. You can also add bullet points, stars or fun bullets by copying and pasting them into your summary from a word document.

Don't forget to add a friendly call to action and asking people to contact by email will help to encourage connections and make you more approachable.

Before completing your personal summary it's definitely worthwhile having a look around at some other profiles in your niche and seeing which ones grab your attention and which ones send you to sleep!

## Experience

This is like your resume, it's important here to add all your positions, education, skills, expertise and responsibilities including any major achievements. Again to make it easier to read you can add bullet points by pasting from a word document.

## Skills and expertise

You can add up to 50 skills to your profile. Once you have added these skills they will be added to your personal profile so when your connections view your profile they will be able to view your skills and they will be offered the opportunity to endorse those skills. Skills with the most endorsements will be listed first. Receiving endorsements is a great way to build your credibility and your professional brand. You can choose not to display any endorsements if you wish.

If people are writing recommendations for you or endorsing certain skills then it is good practice to reciprocate if you agree that they have the skills they have listed.

## Education

You can add all the educational establishments that you attended and all your qualifications together with documents, files, images and videos.

## Visually enhance your profile with videos, images and documents

LinkedIn now gives you the opportunity to showcase your work and experience by adding images, videos and documents to your summary, experience and education section. This is an incredibly powerful way of helping you to tell your story in a visual way. Adding a short and well made video will help to make a more personal connection especially with new connections and help to give them more insight into who you are. A video is also an instant ice breaker and makes it easier for people to remember you. To begin sharing simply click '**Edit**' on your profile and follow the prompts.

## Choosing your most visible and prominent sections

LinkedIn allows you to change the position of the summary, experience, education and skills sections with the arrow you will find to the right of each section. You can select which is the most important section and place it at the top.

## Extras

On the right of your profile in edit mode you can add extra information: Organizations, Honours and Awards, Test Scores, Courses, Patents, Certifications, Volunteering and Causes, Publications, Projects and Languages.

## Edit contact information

In this section you can add one or more twitter accounts, telephone, email, an instant messaging address and up to three web/blog addresses. You can add keyword anchor text to your website address if you wish by choosing 'other' in the drop down list and then adding the keywords that will then become your anchor text.

## Asking for recommendations

A recommendation helps to illustrate your achievements and shows information about why other people have enjoyed working with you. A recommendation is a comment written by another LinkedIn member in their own words to endorse another member. These recommendations matter and can be used by other members when deciding whether or not to do business with you or employ you. Recommendations not only add credibility to your profile ,but according to data, users with recommendations are more likely to appear in searches on LinkedIn.

You can request a recommendation by simply sending a request to another member. Simply click '**Edit Profile**' at the top of the page and a drop down menu will appear, you can then click '**Ask to be recommended**'. You will then be offered a form to complete where you choose the job or education that you want to get recommended for and you are also able to select the connections you want to send your request to. LinkedIn offers a standard message to send with your request, however by adding a personal message and asking your connections to recommend you for something specific, they will be far more likely reply. When they do reply you can choose whether you want to display the recommendation or hide it.

### Customise your public profile URL

When you register LinkedIn will give your personal profile A URL made up of your name and some letters and random numbers. You will find your LinkedIn URL just under your profile picture. You can enhance your personal brand by creating a custom URL which is easier to remember and easier to display on emails and other places where you wish to promote it.

To customise it simply move your cursor over '**Profile**' and then click '**Edit Profile**' then click '**Edit**' next to your URL under your profile picture. On the top right you will see a box '**Your public profile URL**' and you need to click on '**Customise your public profile URL**'. Your URL can contain between 5 and 30 letters and numbers, but no symbols, spaces or special characters. You cannot change more than three times in a six month period.

### Updating your personal profile

If you want to update your personal profile on LinkedIn but do not want your changes and updates to show up in your connections feed, you can temporarily turn off ' **Activity broadcasts**'. Simply click on '**Privacy and Settings**' which is situated on the drop down menu when you click on your photo on the top right of your profile. Then click on '**Turn on/ off your activity broadcasts**' and then remove the tick from the box.

## Viewing your public profile

Your public profile is the profile that can be viewed by people outside LinkedIn. You can view this by clicking '**Edit Profile**' and then click on '**Manage public profile settings**'. LinkedIn allows you to fully control what is displayed on your public profile and you can customise the view if you like and even set it so that none of it is public if you wish. On this page you can also obtain profile badges so that your profile can be viewed on your website, blog or email signature.

# ADDING CONNECTIONS & BUILDING YOUR PERSONAL NETWORK

On LinkedIn your personal network is made up of connections. These connections are called 1st ,2nd and 3rd degree. You can easily identify what type of connection they are as an icon is displayed by their name. You can mage your connections from the '**Network**' tab at the top of your profile.

1st degree connections are those who are directly connected to you and have either sent you an invitation that you have accepted or they have accepted your invitation to connect . 2nd degree connections are those who are connected to your 1st degree connections. 3rd degree connections are a wider network of people connected to your 2nd degree connections. To contact people outside your network you will need to send InMail and this comes with the premium membership.

Once you have successfully set up your profile and company page you will be ready to start making connections. The more connections you have the more chance you have of connecting with a wider network. Here are some tips to building your network:

## Invite Connections.

The quickest and easiest way to add connections is to send an invitation to your email contacts through LinkedIn. To start simply visit your profile home page and click 'Network,' then 'Add Connections'. LinkedIn will take the email that is associated with your account and you will then need to give LinkedIn permission to access your email address book. LinkedIn will match your contacts with those that are already members and then offer you the opportunity to send invitations to those contacts who are not on LinkedIn. Your invitation will include a standard LinkedIn message, but it's definitely beneficial to tailor your message to each individual contact.

You can invite your existing contacts by uploading your own contacts file or by sending out individual invitations. It is recommended that you only send invitations to those people you know well and trust.

You can also send invitations from the 'People you may know' area on the right side of your profile page. Simply click connect next to their name, you can also use LinkedIn search to find people you know. Once they have received and accepted your invitation to connect they will become a '1st degree connection.' Remember every connection you make offers you the potential to connect to even more people.

## Converting 2nd and 3rd degree connections to 1st degree connections

As you become more active on LinkedIn by updating your status, interacting, joining groups and getting to know people you will be able to send out invitations to your 2nd and 3rd connections. Be careful not to send out invitations to people who you do not know as they can report this as spam and LinkedIn only have to be notified a few times and they will close your account.

## Get introduced to 2nd Degree connections

By getting introduced by your 1st degree connections you can reach out to 2nd degree connections. As a free member you can get up to 5 introductions per month and as a premium member you are allowed up to 35 per month, depending on your level of membership. To find people more connections in your niche you can use the advanced search feature. Simply complete the search form and the results will display a list of members and whether you share any connections with those people. Next to where it says 'Connect' there is a down arrow with a drop down menu, simply click on ' **Get introduced**' and you will be shown which of your 1st degree connections have this contact as their 1st degree connection. You can then choose who you wish to introduce you to this new contact and send them a request to be introduced.

### Accept Invitations to connect

The more connections you have the more opportunity you have to expand your network and increase exposure to your brand or personal brand. This is of course up to whether you accept or not, beware though of spammers who quite often stand out because they have not got a complete profile.

### Send a reply when accepting invitations

A great way to break the ice and start building relationships with new connections is to send them a message. The content will obviously depend on how well you know them but this is a great way of keeping the conversation going.

### Find Alumni

You can search who you were at college with by adding the name of the establishment and the years you were there. You can find the 'Alumni tab' under the 'Network' tab.

### Send an InMail

If you are a premium member you are allowed to send between 3 and 25 InMails per month depending on the level of membership you have. This means you do not need to be introduced by a connection and you can reach out to other members directly. In order to get the best response from your InMails make sure your first InMail to a new contact is just a brief enthusiastic and professional introduction of yourself; your goal for your first InMail is just to start a conversation. You could also mention a member that you both have in common. Once you have started the conversation you can then continue the conversation and focus on the benefits you can offer them or how you can help them in some way.

## Use Advanced Search

LinkedIn offers a very sophisticated search facility that lets you find people in specific positions or industries. Premium members can use up to 8 extra advanced search filters.

## Send a message to an Openlink member

Whether or not you are a premium member you can still reach out to any member if they are a member of the Openlink network. If they are part of the Openlink network they will have a badge displayed on their profile or in any search results that they are in. The icon looks like a small ring of dots. You can send a mail by simply clicking **'Send InMail'** on the members profile.

## Share and comment on other peoples posts

Actively contributing to other peoples discussions and status updates is invaluable and can only increase your visibility to your 1st, 2nd and 3rd degree connections.

## Start or join LinkedIn groups

Participating in LinkedIn groups is a very effective way to make new connections. By interacting, commenting and asking questions you can start up new conversations and increase your visibility on LinkedIn.

## Follow other companies

If you follow the company pages of your connections and actively comment and share their content you will increase your visibility to their followers. By supporting their pages they are more likely to participate and share your content.

## Create a post on your Facebook fan page

Announcing your presence on Facebook and inviting your fans to connect with you on LinkedIn will open up new opportunities of connecting with their connections on LinkedIn too.

## Follow up on people you meet

What better way to stay connected with someone you have recently met than by sending them an invitation to connect on LinkedIn when you get back to your office.

## Endorse skills for your connections

Endorsing your 1st degree connection for their skills is are a great way of showing support and recognising them for their expertise. If you give endorsements to your connections they are more likely to reciprocate and also are more likely to think kindly towards you and interact with your content.

## Recommend your connections

Recommending your connections for certain things helps them to win clients and get hired and it also strengthens your relationships with your network. Your connections are more likely to recommend you if you have already recommended them. To recommend simply click on the connection you want to recommend and then click on the down arrow (next to send email) and then click **'Recommend'** You can recommend your connection as a colleague, service provider, business partner or student. You then need to complete the recommendation form and press send. You can recommend someone who is not on LinkedIn too and they will be invited to create a profile on LinkedIn.

You can request recommendations for yourself by going to 'Privacy and Settings' situated in the drop down under your photo on the right and then click on **'Manage Your Recommendations'**

## Post regular updates

Creating conversations and staying engaged with your connections is key to building trust, credibility, building more connections and building your brand. It's a good idea to connect with your audience at least once a day. Being active on LinkedIn will gain you more visibility, when a connection interacts with your updates these actions will be seen by their network which will increase your reach and your potential to gain a new followers.

You can include up to 600 characters in an update and you can include a link or upload a file attachment. Unlike your company page you do not have the opportunity to upload an image file but you can share links and LinkedIn will automatically shorten your links.

Your updates will remain at the top of your profile until it is replaced by another one. When you post an update you can choose who sees your post. You can choose to share your updates with Public and Twitter, just Public or just your 1st degree connections. Only the first 140 characters of your update will show on Twitter.

## Updating your status on your personal profile

LinkedIn is very different to Twitter and Facebook and is purely a professional network and so updates also need to be professional. However, be careful not to overdo the self promotion, as it will just turn your followers off.

Here are some ideas for status updates:
- A description and link to one of your blog articles.
- Update on what you are doing, or ask what others are doing.
- A link to a new blog article that you found interesting and think would appeal to your network.
- A useful quote.
- A link to a pin on Pinterest .
- Tips, advice and useful information about your industry.
- A link to a YouTube video.

- A request to connect on your other social networks.
- An update about your business or press release.
- An update on what you are currently working on.
- Ask a question to spark conversation.
- Share useful online tools you may use to help you with your business.
- Comment on business books you are reading.
- Share posts and articles from top influencers on LinkedIn.

## BENEFITS OF A PREMIUM ACCOUNT

**Benefits of upgrading your account to a premium account.**

The LinkedIn basic account offers many benefits to the user however if you want to use LinkedIn as a sales generation tool and send InMails or allow any member to message you then you will need to upgrade your account to a premium account. LinkedIn offers different premium accounts and you can tailor their services and benefits towards whatever you want to use Linkedin for. You can check your account type in your privacy settings and view the different account types available on the 'compare account types' tab.

- Business - For general business use
- Job Seeker
- Sales Navigator - For sales professionals
- Talent Finder
- Recruiter

Having a premium account can assist you in sourcing new sales leads and finding key decision makers, with its advanced search facility. Premium accounts offer the following features and benefits:

**Custom profile background and larger profile picture**

As a premium member you can now upload a larger profile photo and your own custom header. You can either upload your own branded background or choose from LinkedIn's gallery of background images.

# InMail

InMail allows you to contact users that you are unable to contact with a free account. LinkedIn offers between 3 and 25 InMails per month depending on the subscription type. You don't need any introduction and you can attach your profile with your message when contacting member. If a member does not respond to an InMail within seven days on the eighth day LinkedIn will credit you with an additional InMail. You can purchase additional InMails too. You can check your InMail status in 'Privacy and Settings'.

## Stand out on search results

As a premium member you will stand out in search results and your profile will be displayed twice as large as non premium members.

## More search results

As a premium member you can get more search results, up to 700 contacts depending on the membership you have. You can also save more searches and more alerts if there are new people who have fallen into the search criteria of your saved searches. To access your saved searches simply visit the advanced search and click on the gear icon on the top right of the page. With premium membership you can make your searches even more specific with up to eight advanced search filters.

## Keyword suggestions

LinkedIn will give you top keyword suggestions for your profile summary which are optimised and will help you to get found more easily in search.

## Who's viewed my profile

You can see who has viewed your profile on the right side of your homepage. As a paid member you can view the profile of anyone who has viewed your profile in the last 90 days. If you do not have a paid option you can only view up to five profiles and see the number people have viewed your profile in the last 90 days.

## Premium badge

As a premium member you can display a badge that shows to other members you are a premium member. You can choose to display this or not. This can be found on your 'Privacy & Settings' tab. Badges are displayed on your profile and in search results.

## Openlink

The Openlink network allows any member to contact you by InMail completely free whether they are a premium member or not. Openlink opens you up to more networking opportunities and lets other professionals know that you do not mind them reaching out to you. You can choose whether you want to be included on the Openlink network or not. If you want to be part of this network then you need to display the Openlink badge on your profile, this option can be found on your 'Premium Badge Settings' and the badge looks like a small ring of dots.

## Lead Builder

The Lead builder is available with the premium account for sales professionals and allows you to create and save lists of prospective customers using more advanced search criteria. You can find lead builder when you click on '**Advanced**' next to the search bar.

## THINGS YOU NEED TO KNOW

**LinkedIn 'Contacts' and organising your contacts and connections.**
LinkedIn Contacts is a feature that is available to all members and allows you to organize your contacts in one place. When you click on '**Contacts**' from your 'Network' tab you will see a list of your connections and also you may see photos of your connections who have birthdays or a have a new job or photos of the people you have set reminders to contact. In 'Contacts' you can add profiles that you have saved and add more information to these profiles. This information can only be viewed by you. You can view your contacts however you want by pulling them up

based on different criteria. For example you could pull up members with the same tags or pull up your connections only.

You can add contact information, notes and details about how you met. You can also add information and tags. Tags are simply keywords that help you organize your contacts. You can also set reminders for yourself to contact and stay in touch with a connection or contact.

## Pulse

LinkedIn Pulse is a source of professional news which is tailored to you and it is where you can discover and share compelling content related to the topics you are interested in, or the industry you are in. Updates and articles from the influencers you follow will appear in your updates feed. You can choose which Channels or Influencers you wish to follow. Simply go to the 'Interests' tab and select **'Pulse'** and then **'All Influencers'** or **'All Channels'**

## Restrictions to using Linkedin

LinkedIn does enforce their terms of service and if members do not adhere to them they can be restricted. This can happen if you send one too many invitations that are marked as spam, or a number of users have indicated that they do not know you. This can happen quite easily and LinkedIn will often remove the restriction if it's your first time. You need to visit the help centre and type in 'Account Restricted' to have this restriction lifted.

To avoid being restricted do not send invitations to people you have had no contact with and if you want to connect, then send a personalized introduction message first by InMail and then ask them if it is ok to send them an invite to connect. Don't send one unless they reply.

## The Help Centre

LinkedIn provides a wealth of information about their network. You can find out anything about LinkedIn simply by accessing the help centre which can be found on the menu under your profile picture on the top right of your profile.

## CHAPTER FOUR

### CREATING YOUR COMPANY PROFILE ON LINKEDIN

LINKEDIN OFFERS AN incredibly effective platform for promoting your business and your products with company pages. Company pages perform very well in searches for company searches on Linkedin and there are huge opportunities for generating leads. Once you have set up your company page you can post updates directly from you company page to your followers and like and comment as your company too. You can showcase your products and services or other content, generate social recommendations, send traffic to your website and generate leads.

As long as you have your own a domain email address then you can create a company page on LinkedIn. Simply move your cursor over 'Interests' on the top of the page and then click on '**Companies**' and then click '**Add a Company**' and simply add your company name and email address and then LinkedIn will send you an email so that they can verify your company.

When creating your description it will need to be optimised for both LinkedIn search and Google Search. Google displays up to 156 characters of your description, so you need to make the beginning of your description includes the facts which are going to be useful to your ideal customer. You can add your website and company specialities and your logo and a company homepage image. Since your 'about' section will be situated at the bottom of your page it's a good idea to add a message to your homepage image.

Here are the image sizes for your images which can be PNG/JPEG/

GIF format:

- **Company Homepage Image** - Minimum 646 x 220
- **Company Standard Logo** – 100 x 60 ( Image will be resized to fit)
- **Company Square Logo** 50 x 50 ( Image will be resized to fit)
- **Product pictures** 100 X 80 pixels

## CREATING A SHOWCASE PAGE

If your business is quite complex and has multiple products and you want to deliver different messages to different audiences then showcase pages can be incredibly useful. However before you look at setting one up you need to work out if they are really going to benefit your business, as it will take more resources to build separate audiences and it may be that your company page is sufficient for your needs. Showcase pages are dedicated pages that let you segment and deliver multiple brand messages to specific audiences. You can create up to ten showcase pages and they work in a similar way to company pages, you can advertise your showcase page and analyze your performance with LinkedIn analytics.

Creating a showcase page is very straight forward. Simply go to your company page and then click on the down arrow next to the 'Edit' button on your company page and then click 'Create Showcase Page'. You need to create a showcase name, add a page description ( 75 to 200 characters), a showcase website URL, your industry and upload images as follows:

Hero Image Minimum: 974 X 330 Pixels
Logo: 100 X 60 pixels. Image will be resized to fit.
Square logo: 50 x 50 pixels. Image will be resized to fit.

Your showcase page will display any other company showcase pages and will show that your showcase is part of your company page.

## CREATING A SPONSORED UPDATE

Sponsored updates work similarly to promoted posts on Facebook and let you promote your company updates to targeted users who are not yet following your company page, allowing you to grow your reach and build awareness. They can be used for lead generation or to promote an event, a blog post, a new product or a giveaway that you are using to build your opt-in. Before you decide to promote your post, make sure you have a clear objective in mind. If your objective is to drive engagement then it's a good idea to see how your update is performing without promotion and then if you think it is doing well, sponsor it. Here are some tips for your sponsored update:

- Keep to one specific topic with one URL.
- Use a compelling image.
- Create a compelling headline.
- Make sure you have a good landing page with your offer an opt-in sign up form if you are looking to grow your subscribers.

To create a sponsored post simply create and post your update as normal and then click on '**Sponsor update**' under the post. You will then be taken to another page where you can choose to either '**Create an ad**' or '**Sponsor an update**'

Select '**Sponsor an update**' and then name your campaign and select the company page and the update you wish to sponsor. You will then be taken to another page where you can select the audience you want from the following criteria; location, companies and job title. You then to select your budget and then 'Save'. You can pay for sponsored updates based on the number of members who see your update ( CPM) or the number of clicks they receive (CPC).

Once you campaign is up and running you view the performance of your sponsored update in '**Analytics**' which will show you the following:

- **Impressions** The number of times each update was shown to members
- **Clicks** The number of clicks on your company name, logo or

your content.

- **Interactions** The number of times people have liked, commented on, and shared.
- **Engagement %** The number of interactions and the number of clicks and followers gained, divided by the number of impressions.
- **Followers Acquired** How many followers you gained by promoting each update.
- **Reach** A graph displaying the number of times your updates were seen organically and through paid campaigns on a daily basis.
- **Engagement** A graph displaying the number of times members clicked, liked or commented and shared your content both organically and through paid campaigns.

## BUILDING YOUR AUDIENCE ON YOUR COMPANY PAGE

In order to drive engagement on your company page you will need to build your followers. LinkedIn has stated that you need at least one hundred and fifty followers to drive engagement. Here are some tactics to attract and gain followers for your page.

### Adding Social Plugins to your sites

To enable users to share your content and add follow buttons for your website or blog you can find the code at this page https:// developer.linkedin.com/plugins

- **The Follow Button** Adding the company follow button to your website will assist you in growing your LinkedIn company page community so you can engage with your target audience, develop relationships, and acquire leads. By simply clicking the Follow Company button, users will automatically begin following your company page. Status updates you post from your company page will now show up on your follower's homepage feed. By encouraging your audience to like and share and interact with your content you will be spreading the word to their followers as well.

- **The Member Profile Plug in** You can also bring your LinkedIn member profile to your site. This immediately adds a personal touch to your website and you helps to promote your own personal brand.
- **Share Button** 'InShares' are a bit like Facebook 'likes' and twitter 'retweets' Using the share button allows professionals to share your valuable content among their connections and when people share your content it is added to the Linkedin ecosystem, and your content is shown to those who are interested in this type of content. This will offer you more visibility and more traffic from professionals.
- **The Recommend Plugin** This plugin enables users to recommend your products and services to LinkedIn's professional audience, and drive traffic back to your site.

## Post regular updates to your company page

Encourage lively interaction on your page by regularly posting valuable and interesting content to your company page. Content creation is covered in more depth later on in the book.

## Invite your friends, family and co-workers

Inviting the people you already have a relationship with is a good way to start to build your initial following and to encourage engagement.

## Run an email invitation campaign

Inviting your current contacts and opt-in subscribers to your company page is yet another way to stay in contact and build relationships and more trust with those contact.

## Announce to your connections

Once you have created your company page you can post an update on your personal profile announcing that your company page is up and invite your connections to follow.

## Announce your company page on your other social networks

Inviting your followers from other social platforms to join the conversation will often appeal to your followers as it's an additional way for them to interact and make new connections as well.

## Participate in LinkedIn Groups or create one

Participating in groups is a powerful way to drive people to your company page and promote your brand. You can mention your company page as long as it has useful information that is relevant to any group discussion taking place. Creating your own group can be a very powerful way of promoting your company page on LinkedIn.

## Promote your page with Linkedin ads

LinkedIn offers targeted advertising opportunities. Your adverts can appear throughout LinkedIn and you can target your adverts to members in specific industries, companies and regions. The ability to target people with certain job titles makes LinkedIn advertising even more effective. Once these targeted members become followers or interact with your content on your company page then their connections will see these action widening your reach further.

To advertise simply click on **'Business Services'** from your home page and then select **'Advertising'** and you can choose from **'Create an ad'** and **'Sponsoring an update'**. You can use text, images or videos and you can set your budget and stop your ads at any time.

## Follow other companies

If you follow other businesses on LinkedIn then those businesses may very well reciprocate and follow you back. Once you start interacting with these pages other members may come and check out your company page. Please note that you can only follow a page as an individual and not a company.

## Employees

Ask your employees to create their own personal profile which is linked to the company as their employer, this way you will increase the reach of your business. Once they have linked then they automatically become profiles that can follow your page, comment, like and share your posts.

## Add your company page link to all your content

Make it easy for people to interact with your company page by adding it to all your content, white papers, pdf's and email signatures.

## Post updates to your personal profile

Encourage your connections to follow your company page by posting occasional details about your business on your personal profile. This is especially effective if you have an image and a link to a useful article on your website or blog.

## Follow your connections

When you make a new connection and then follow their business they may well reciprocate and follow your page.

## Consider upgrading to a paid account

You may at this stage decide that upgrading to a paid account is going to give you additional contact options for building more connections.

# CHAPTER FIVE

## CONTENT IS KING ON LINKEDIN

IN ORDER TO build a thriving community of brand advocates and customers who want to share your content, sign up to your newsletter and buy your products you are going to need to build trust, loyalty and likeability. The only way to do this is by communicating with them on regular basis in the right way and by consistently delivering the highest possible quality content which will grab their attention, appeal to their interests and add real value to their lives. Once your followers start engaging with your content, you will start building trust and start converting them into customers.

Content really is king on LinkedIn and in order to create the right content, you are going to need to have a real understanding of your target audience and deep insight into what interests and motivates them. Once you have this information and put this together with the strategies in this book there is no reason why you cannot build a thriving community of advocates for your brand on Linkedin. In this chapter you are going to learn about the different types of post, different types of content and tips on how help you create the best experience for your connections and followers so you can receive the highest engagement.

## 31 IDEAS FOR CREATING CONTENT ON LINKEDIN

You may be wondering how you are going to consistently produce and deliver compelling content to your audience on a regular basis for the foreseeable future. However once you have picked your topic of interest you will surprised how one idea will lead to another and you will be able to find numerous pieces of content to create and post. When you post your status updates on your company page your followers will see these updates on their homepage feed and they can comment, like or share your content. Your aim here is to amplify your message in order to grow your following. The more actions that your followers take with your content the more likely your page will be seen by other Linkedin members. According to Linkedin this type of engagement on company pages is responsible for over a third of impressions. Here are some ideas for content that can be adapted to any type of business or topic:

## 1. Relatable content

Relatable content is one of the best types of content and one of the most shared types of content. Relatable content is anything that your target audience can relate to and identify with, it's when your audience sees a piece of content and immediately thinks, "Yes, I can relate to that and this is exactly the way I feel when this happens". It's incredibly powerful because this content is immediately communicating to your audience that you understand them and you feel their pain or joy and you can empathise with them. With relatable content you are communicating with them on quite a deep level which all helps to build relationships and trust. This is why Someecards is so successful, most of their content is relatable.

## 2. Emotive content

Evoking an emotional response is an essential ingredient to successful viral content marketing. If you create content that evokes a strong positive emotional response it will help your audience associate that emotion with your brand. Content like this is very memorable and if you can make people feel something by posting an image, text or a video, this can really help in building your brand and creating powerful associations. Evoking any of the primary emotions be it surprise, joy, fear, sadness, anger or disgust is a certain way to get people sharing your content.

### 3. Educational content

Posting informative content about your subject is invaluable, this will help you to stand out as a thought leader and expert in your field. If your content is valuable and useful then your followers are likely to keep coming back for more and are likely to share your content too. Remember your audience are also looking to find and share valuable content with their friends and customers and will want to be associated with any compelling content you create.

### 4. Informative

This could be about letting your followers know about something that is happening, like a Webinar, a trade show or an event in the area, or a special offer, or any information that will be of use or value to them.

### 5. Entertaining/amusing content

Social media is all about being social and having fun, people love sharing funny stuff. Even if you did not create it yourself but you think it is going to appeal to your target audience then share it. The aim here is to amuse and entertain your audience, humor is a winner all round and not only does humor break down barriers it is also more likely to be liked and shared.

### 6. Seasonal Content

Posting content relating to important holidays and annual celebrations is a really good way to stay connected with your audience. If you have an international audience then being aware of their holidays and religious celebrations will go a long way to building relationships.

### 7. Inspiring and motivational content

The truth is everyone has a bad day sometimes and needs a little bit of motivation or cheering up. A motivational quote will help to lift your audience and can really help to connect with them. If you know what your audience wants, what they aspire to and what their frustrations are, then it is likely that you will be able to motivate them by posting content which inspires them. These types of post are also very shareable especially if put together with a colourful and inspiring image like a cartoon or photo.

## 8. Employee and behind the scenes content

If you have news about your employees and the great things they are doing then post it. Maybe they have been involved in a fundraiser or they have won an employee of the month award. Giving your audience a behind the scenes view of your business helps to keep your business and brand looking real and authentic and adds human interest.

## 9. Customer Content

Having a member of the month or including news or content about a customer's business is a great way to spark interest in your posts. Sharing a customer's content not only shows you value your audience but can also encourage them to do the same. If you are B2B you could also invite your audience to network and let them share their page on your page once a month or once a week. This is a great way to offer them value, it also creates loyalty, keeps your page in their mind and keeps them coming back again and again to visit your page.

## 10. Shared Content

Whilst it's great to post most of your own content, don't be afraid to share other peoples content as long as it is relevant. The more valuable content you share, the more valuable you will become to your audience and the more likely they will keep coming back for more. Sharing content is also incredibly important in building relationships with your followers, they are going to be far more open to your brand if you are supporting their's.

## 11. Statistics

People love statistics which relate to their niche. If your business is B2B then posting statistics can gain a great deal of interest especially if they are displayed in a visually appealing way, for instance with an infographic or graph. These are often shared if they are translated into a useful tip for your followers.

## 12. Questions

Asking questions about subjects that your audience may be interested in is a great way to encourage comments, interaction and community. People love to share their opinions and thoughts and they love the opportunity to communicate, contribute and be heard. Even if you are posting an image or video it's good practice to ask a question.

## 13. Top Ten lists

People love lists about who or what is top or best. Lists spark interest and this is most probably because people like to compare their choices and judgement with others. Some may like to see that their opinions match others and feel they are right in that choice or others may feel comforted by the fact their choices are not the same and they are unique.

## 14. Controversial

Posting a controversial statement can spark great conversation and interaction, remember people love to voice their opinions, have an input and be heard. It may be a good idea to stay out of the discussion here as you do not want to lose followers and you need to be sensitive to your audience in order not to upset them so be careful with what topics you pick.

## 15. Special offers

Social media is a great way to get the message out about the special offers you have running, but you will need to be careful not to post them too often or they just appear like advertising and bad noise in your audience's news feed. You need to make sure that what you are offering is of real value, that it is exclusive to your followers and you are set a deadline to redeem the offer.

## 16. Contests

Running a contest is a great way to generate leads and widen your reach on LinkedIn. If you want to use LinkedIn to run a competition you will need to create a Landing page outside LinkedIn to house your rules and entry details. It is very important for you to look into the rules governing contests in your state or country, often using a third party application to run your competition can be a very good idea.

## 17. Member feedback

Asking your followers their advice, or for feedback on a new product is a great way to create engagement and also makes your audience feel they are valued.

## 18. Tips and tricks

Offering a weekly or daily 'Top Tip' can keep your audience hooked and returning again and again for the latest information and are a great way to increase loyalty and build relationships. Tips can be anything from instructions on how to do something to information about a useful app.

## 19. News and current events

Offering information about the latest news in your area or industry is a certain way to keep people interested and sharing your content. Being current and up to date with local news is really useful to your audience and it keeps your business looking fresh and cutting edge. To keep up to date with news, subscribe to news feeds and blogs that offer news on your industry or your local area.

## 20. Negative content

People always like to hear about what not to do, for example: 'Ten Things not to do on a first date' or 'Ten things not to say in a job interview', the list of possibilities for this type of post are endless and can create a great deal of amusement and interest.

## 21. Music if you are a musician

If you are a band and want to promote your music then there is no better way to promote your material than by posting links to your music and videos on LinkedIn.

## 22. Q & A live session

You can host a live question and answers session on your page. This is a really good way to create conversation and engagement. It also creates a professional, informative and caring image. You can do this by allotting and promoting a specific time for followers to post their questions in the comment section of your LinkedIn update. Or you could choose to ask them to post their questions and give them a day when you will be answering them, this way you get more time to research if you need to. In both cases it's a good idea to post an image promoting the session.

## 23. Broadcast live

By using an application called Livestream you can broadcast any live event to almost any social destination. You can also watch, like and share any event that may be of interest to your audience.

## 24. Fill in the blanks posts

Getting your audience involved with your content is a very powerful way of creating engagement. 'Fill in the blank' posts can be a way of creating engagement and conversation, for example:

I love going to _____ on my holidays because…

My Monday morning must have _____

I always take _____ on holiday.

## 25. Caption this

Posting a photo and then asking your audience to caption it is a really effective and light hearted way to drive engagement and you could also turn this into a contest. You can use images from stock photo sites or sites like Flickr Creative Commons, make sure to choose images that will provoke interest and are humorous or inspiring.

## 26. Case studies

Case studies are a really effective way to demonstrate how something works with real examples. You can use case studies to show how your customers have used your products or services to benefit them in some way. You can also use them to demonstrate a principle or method of doing something by using other businesses as examples.

## 27. Internet Memes

Meme comes from the greek word 'mimema' which means something imitated. An internet meme is a style, action or idea which spreads virally across the internet. They can take the form of images, videos or hashtags. There are plenty of tools and apps out there to help you create memes such as www.memegen.com and imgur.com which are popular ones.

## 28. Like versus share votes

This involves combining two competing images in one post and then asking your audience to vote for which image they prefer by liking or sharing. This is a really quick way to expand your reach and get your brand out there. To be successful at this you really need to have good subject and one that most people identify with.

## 29. Your blog

Creating regular blog posts is a very effective way of getting your followers onto your website or blog. Make sure you always include an image to provoke interest and asking a question can create intrigue and curiosity.

## 30. Greetings

Simply posting an attractive image or a wishing your followers good morning, good night or to enjoy their weekend will go a long way in breaking the ice and building relationships. These types of posts help to make positive associations with your brand.

## 31. Testimonials

You may have received a review on your website or Google Places or simply a message from someone. Posting about good things that people write or say about you contributes to your social proof and builds trust. Remember people will believe more about what others say about your business than what you as the owner says about it.

## THE DIFFERENT TYPES OF MEDIA AVAILABLE

In order to create the best experience for you followers and connections you are going to need to create a good balance of content using the different variety of posts available to you. LinkedIn offers you the opportunity to post text, images and links to SlideShare presentations, videos, blog posts and websites.

## Images

'A picture paints a thousand words'

If you are already a LinkedIn user then you probably know that an image grabs your attention more than any other post in your newsfeed. This is because most of us are visually wired and most of us can identify with an image much more quickly than text. Statistics prove that pictures get more comments, shares and likes than any other post and that your followers are far more likely to click on a link to a website or blog or to watch a video if your post contains a picture. Even though you cannot post images on your personal profile, you can post them on your company page and then share them on your profile. If you are posting a link to your blog or an article on your website then make sure you include a compelling image, you are far more likely to gain interest this way. Images not only get shared more they also have huge viral potential, get remembered and also create an emotional connection with your audience.

You don't have to be an expert photographer, you can find images from stock photos and also free sites like flickr (be careful to check the licence and what you are allowed to do with the images in terms of changing or adding text, etc.) Adding text can be achieved by using photoshop or other online graphic design apps which are available online and are easy to use like www.picmonkey.com . Some stock photo sites also offer you the functionality to add effects and text to your images.

## Videos

As with images, video is highly shareable, has a huge viral potential and increases engagement. People love videos and a good video can offer a huge amount of entertainment, make learning more interesting, more fun and easier to understand. Videos are also great at helping to build relationships, trust and rapport with your audience and there really is no better way of introducing yourself and building a personal connection with your audience than with video.

The type of videos you should be posting on LinkedIn are educational, informative and entertaining and while there is room for the occasional product video these really belong on your website or blog.

## Text

Whether you are posting a text only post, an image or a video, it is likely that you will be including some text to either introduce or describe your post. As a general rule of thumb the shorter you keep it the more engagement you will receive. Whilst that is not to say that longer posts are unsuccessful, generally speaking it is best to keep the majority of your posts shorter.

While images are definitely more effective and receive higher engagement there is still room for text only images to deliver the occasional tip, a greeting or to ask a question.

## LinkedIn Long-Form-Posts

Soon to be available to all LinkedIn members long form posts which allow you to create long posts on LinkedIn's publishing platform and share them with your network. You can add photos and videos and edit and delete your posts as and when you require. If your posts are shared by your network they can reach a wider audience and anyone outside your network can follow you from your post and receive your updates too.

## Blog posts

According to research 70% of consumers click through to a website from a retail blog. Blogs are nearly essential now for any business who wants to get found on the internet and social media is another very effective tool to drive traffic to your blog. If you do not have a blog then you need to seriously consider creating one. There are numerous free and paid blogging platforms available and there is a whole chapter covering this subject later on in the book.

## Infographics and diagrams

Infographics provide a fascinating way to present statistical information. They are engaging, very shareable, have huge viral potential and make figures look far more interesting and are easier to understand than a list of numbers. People love statistical information relating to their interest because it helps to confirm or affirm what they already may believe and helps to give them more confidence in what they are doing or selling. You do not have to be an expert graphic designer to create infographics there are numerous applications available on the web which can help you create infographics.

## Podcasts

Podcasting is a type of digital media usually comprising a series of audio, radio or video files. You can subscribe to podcasts as you can to blogs and newsletters. For example if you download a podcast on itunes, every time the author produces a new one, itunes will automatically download it. As with video podcasts are effective at helping to build trust with the listener and can also help to make you stand out as an authority or influencer in your niche. They also encourage customer loyalty if they are produced on a weekly or very regular basis and are incredibly handy for people who are on the go and want to listen while travelling to work or on the way to a meeting. LinkedIn is to the ideal place to promote your podcast.

## Cartoons

Cartoons work very well with humor and relatable content. Posting cartoons that your audience can relate to can help demonstrate that you understand and identify with them, they are a great ice breaker and highly shareable as well. Once shared they are very likely to appeal to more of your target audience and are a great way to widen your reach. If you have an idea for a cartoon and you are not an artist them there are sites like Fiverr.com that offer creative services at very reasonable prices.

## SlideShare

SlideShare is primarily a slide sharing site but you can upload powerpoint, keynote, pdf and open office presentations. SlideShare is a great way to communicate your message and very straight forward and easy to use. It is also another way to get your content rated, commented on and shared and your presentations can be embedded into LinkedIn and your website or blog.

## Ebooks & PDF Documents

Turning your content into an ebook is a great way to present your content and offering a free ebook is a really good way to build your opt-in lists and gives your reader something of great value.

## Webinars

A Webinar is like an interactive online conference or workshop. Webinars are a great way of interacting with your audience and building relationships. They can be used for presenting and training, selling a programme or course, or answering questions from your audience. They can be saved and listened to at a later date for anyone who could not make the date and time. Using LinkedIn to announce your Webinar is a very effective way to promote your online event and get people to sign up.

## TIPS FOR POSTING ON LINKEDIN

### Post frequently

The number of posts you create will depend on the amount of valuable content you have, but anything between 1-5 times per day is optimal. According to LinkedIn, statistical information updates which are posted in the morning receive up to 45% more engagement.

### Headlines and Descriptions

Make sure your headlines are attention grabbing and your descriptions are brief and to the point. Try and include a question or a call to action wherever possible.

### Questions

People are on LinkedIn to interact and get noticed so they will interact with other members if given the opportunity. One of the best ways to encourage this interaction is through asking questions. These could be questions relating to business or other interests. Questions are great ice breakers, spark conversation and increase engagement. Whether posting an image, video or text, asking a question will provoke discussion and engagement.

### Include a Link

Wherever possible include a link to an external blog, website or document.

### Include an image

Try and include a compelling image in your post wherever possible. Images attract more attention and interest than plain text and are more likely to get shared and commented on.

### Pin to top

LinkedIn allows you to highlight your most important updates at the top of your page. It's a good idea to put your most popular post here or a post regarding your latest offer, promotion or event that you want to promote.

### Is this relevant to my audience?

Every time you post anything ask yourself this question and if the answer is no then don't post it.

### Sponsored updates

To increase your reach and to promote specific offers or events use sponsored updates.

### Schedule posts

Hootsuite and Buffer allows you post directly to your personal profile and your company page from your dashboard.

### Follow your company page

Make sure you add yourself as a follower of your company page so you can share updates on your personal profile.

## BENEFIT FROM LINKEDIN'S PUBLISHING PLATFORM

As a member you will be shortly able to publish long-form-posts on LinkedIn's publishing platform. LinkedIn are slowly rolling out the new publishing platform to all its members. This does not mean that you become a LinkedIn influencer but your post will become part of your professional profile and can be viewed in the posts section of your profile. You can share your posts with your connections and they can like, comment and share your posts which will help to distribute your post beyond your network. If other members outside your network see your post they can also choose to follow you from your long form post and receive updates when you publish another post. Long-form-posts are public and are searchable both on and off LinkedIn so even non members will be able to see you posts.

To create a long-form-post simply go to your 'Share an update' box and then click the pencil icon and it will take you to the publishing tool. You can add links, visuals and embed videos. Once your post has been created you can edit it or delete it if you wish, and you can view stats for your long form post as well.

To view your posts simply click 'Profile' at the top of your page and then find the 'Posts' section and then click any of your posts and then click 'See your posts and stats'. You can choose to hide or flag any abusive comments.

Long-form-posts are all about sharing your professional expertise. If you want your posts to get distributed beyond your network then you need to stay away from promotional posts and keep your posts centred around creating value for your audience. LinkedIn determines quality of posts by their algorithm and other factors and some high quality posts may get tagged and distributed through LinkedIn Pulse and emails but there is no guarantee of this.

Here are some tips for creating long-form-posts
- Keep your posts relevant to your expertise and around subjects that your target audience are interested in.
- Share your posts on other networks, such as Twitter, Facebook and Google+, You can automatically share with Twitter by checking the Twitter icon on the publishing tool.
- Share your posts with relevant LinkedIn Groups.
- Publish frequently.
- Engage on the platform by liking and commenting on other member posts.
- Include an image wherever possible to add to the visual experience.
- Ask a question at the end of your post to encourage discussion and engagement.
- Grow your following so you can increase your reach.

## CHAPTER SIX

## *LINKEDIN GROUPS*

LINKEDIN GROUPS OFFER a place for their members who are in the same industry or niche to share information, share content, make connections, network and post job vacancies. As a member of LinkedIn you can join up to 50 groups at one time and after that you would have to withdraw from one in order to join another. However, even though you can join up to 50 groups this may spread you very thin and being very active in a just few groups maybe a better use of your resources than trying to participate in many.

LinkedIn Groups offer you the opportunity to:
- Connect and interact with other members
- Join discussions
- Share your knowledge and build authority, influence and credibility
- Become a top influencer
- Source information and increase your knowledge
- Expand your reach and find followers for your company page, your website or blog.

However LinkedIn Groups should not be used to blatantly promote your product or service.

## *JOINING A GROUP*

One of the advantages of joining a group is that members appear in the search results of that group. So if you go to a group and click the number stating how many members the groups has you can see whether any of your connections are already members.

To find groups simply click 'Interests' on the top menu of your profile and then click 'Groups' on the drop down menu. You will then be able to search groups under keywords that you enter and start filtering and viewing results. You can view 'Open Groups' without joining but you can only view content of 'member only groups' after you have joined.

There are over a million groups on LinkedIn so you can afford to be selective when choosing the groups you want to join. Before joining, you need to work out what your goals are, are they to build connections and relationships or to gain knowledge from key influencers or to establish yourself as a thought leader? If your main goal is to drive traffic to a website or blog then you need to find groups that allow you to post links.

When searching for groups you can view a description of each group together with the group statistics which include the number of members and the number of discussions and comments that have been made. Joining smaller, lively groups with lots of interaction may be more advantageous than joining larger ones with little activity, this is where quality can sometimes outweigh quantity. The demographics are important too, joining a group when the majority of its members are international maybe a complete waste of time for you if you are a local business. Viewing the groups activity feed will help you see whether the group relevant to you or not and whether you think you could be able to contribute in some way.

Once you have made your selection and joined you can then introduce yourself and start commenting and joining in with discussions. If you want to build influence then it is important to stay active and engage with members and contribute to discussions. LinkedIn keeps track of the interaction that takes place in groups and appoints 'The Top Influencers of the week'. You can view 'The Top Influencers' at the top right of the group page, these are the people who have contributed and participated in discussions and liked and commented the most. This is a huge opportunity for exposure for you and your brand if you are appointed.

## LinkedIn Discussions

LinkedIn discussions are a great way to communicate with others in your niche and build connections. To start a discussion simply hit the 'Discussion' link at the top and add the title for your discussion and a description. You can add an article or ask a question. You can also post relevant content with a link to your company page, website or blog and you can post this to your group and Twitter if you like. Your group may also have a special section for adding promotions and jobs.

You can participate in discussions by liking and commenting and you can also follow a particular discussion. You can choose to be notified by email whenever anyone comments on that particular discussion.

## Starting a poll

LinkedIn allows you to start a poll which is an effective method of driving engagement and shows that you are interested in people's opinions rather than just self promotion. To start a poll simply click 'Discussions' and then click the poll icon for when your poll expires.

## Promotions

If the group allows, you can post promotions which are visible to the group for up to 14 days.

## Group Settings

When you click on the 'i' button on the top right of the group you can find out all about the group and also you can manage your settings. Here you can also manage whether you want an email to be sent to you for every activity within the group or whether or not you want to allow other members to send you messages.

## Member only groups

Member only groups have a padlock displayed next to the group name and are groups that can only be seen by other members. They can only be seen by the group members and they will not appear in search.People often create closed groups for their customers and use them as a forum.

## Don't get SWAM'ed

SWAM stands for 'Site Wide Auto Moderation'. If you are SWAM'ed it means that all your posts and comments are not posted automatically and have to be approved by the group owner before it can be made visible. This can happen if a group owner marks your posts as 'requires moderation' or you get blocked from a group. LinkedIn have introduced this to limit the abuse of groups on the platform.

If you are SWAM'ed then your posting privileges will be limited across all LinkedIn groups and not just the group where you were SWAM'ed. Make sure you read the rules for all the groups you join and then adhere to those rules. If you do get SWAM'ed the only thing you can do is write to the group owner or write to LinkedIn customer support asking them to reconsider.

## THE BENEFITS FOR STARTING YOUR OWN GROUP

Creating your own group on LinkedIn has a multitude of benefits particularly if you are B2B. Here are some of the benefits you can enjoy by creating your own group on LinkedIn:

## Raises your profile

As a group creator your name will be clearly featured as the owner of the group and running a successful group will help you to be considered as a thought leader. The more you contribute to your group by interacting and offering valuable content the more you will build your credibility and be considered as an expert in your niche.

## Lets you send weekly emails to your members

As a group creator you can send emails to your members every week. This is a great opportunity to gain attention by sending your members the links to your top quality content relating to the group subject.

## Drives traffic to your website or blog

You can drive traffic in a few ways:

- Adding your URL to the group profile is great exposure as most people will click on this link when deciding whether or not to join the group.
- Include your URL in the groups welcome message.
- Include your URL when sending valuable content to your members once a week.
- By creating discussions within the group and including your URL.

## Creates community

Many people love to be part of a community and join other like minded people in discussions. If you are the creator of a thriving LinkedIn group and community by bringing people together and helping them make connections you will be looked on very favourably by your members. In turn this will create trust and good will towards you and your brand.

## Expands your personal network

Creating a group is a great way to build connections. If your group is active then members are going to want to connect with you because you are the authority and you are likely to receive numerous invitations to connect on LinkedIn.

## Generates leads and sales

When you send out your initial welcome email and thank members for joining you can include details and benefits of joining the group and also a brief background and description of yourself and your business. You could also invite them to join your newsletter or invite them to connect on other social networks.

## BEFORE YOU CREATE A GROUP ON LINKEDIN

Actually creating a group is very straight forward, however before you going ahead and create one you should realize that growing and managing a successful takes huge commitment and can be quite extremely time consuming. Here are some things you need to do and take into consideration before creating a group on LinkedIn:

### Join other groups.

Joining and involving yourself in groups which are managed by others is a great way of getting to know how groups work. By joining popular and active groups you will see what the group administrators are doing to make it so successful and see how you can adapt ideas to your group to bring value to your members.

### Consider your resources

Do you have the resources required to manage and administer an active group? As well as posting discussions and creating content you will also need to approve members and regularly monitor the group so you do not get spammers and irrelevant discussions being posted by others. You may need to allocate a number of staff members to administer the group. If the group is not managed properly this will actually work against your brand.

### Define and set your goals

You will need to look closely at your overall marketing goals for your business and see whether creating a group is the best way of achieving those goals in comparison to other methods. The topic needs to be specific but also wide enough to allow for unlimited content creation and discussion. There is huge amount of competition out there and in order to attract high quality members then it needs to be really original. When choosing your topic or subject you will need to consider the following:

- What subjects are going to offer your target audience the most value?
- What subjects are going to help you best achieve your goals?

- Are there other groups about this subject? And if so, is there room to create another group and can you bring more value than the current group/groups?
- How you can make your group unique?

## Create an excellent plan

When your group is running you will need to aim to post at least one discussion per week with related content and you will need to decide on whether you are going to allow others to post discussions and content or just comment. You will also need to plan the announcements that you are going to send out once a week, the content you are going to include and work out how you are going to generate leads from these announcements without being too self promotional.

## Build a landing page or website for your group

Creating a landing page about your group on your website or even creating a website for your group is essential. This way you can offer members something of value in return for their name and email addresses. Even though you are permitted to send out an announcement to your group members every week you will not have access to their email addresses. Having these email contacts will give you control over how you can connect with your members.

## Search Groups

Before creating your group, search the groups section to see how other groups are listed and what makes certain groups stand out. Make sure you use the search feature at the top of your homepage as opposed to the group directory, this way you will be able to search by type and see the way the groups are listed. The group directory will only show you groups listed alphabetically.

## CREATING A GROUP ON LINKEDIN

To create your group simply click '**Interests**' then select **'Groups'** and then '**Create a group**' Here are some tips for creating your group:

## Your Group Logo

You can create your own logo for the group and you can upload a PNG, JPEG or GIF image. The logo will appear as a thumbnail beside the group name, on the group search page and on the top right of the actual group page. When creating your custom logo try and keep it in line with your corporate branding and, as it is quite small try, and make it as striking as possible without too much text.

## Your group name

Your group name will be displayed in bold together with your summary and logo in the search results page. Your group name is very important and offers you the opportunity to be unique and also to get found within LinkedIn. You will need to consider what keywords your target audience are going to be searching for when looking to join a group, these key words are what are going to drive your results in the LinkedIn search so you will need to try and include these in your name. Be careful not to use a famous name or a trade mark or your name will be taken away from you and you could open yourself up to a legal headache.

## Select your group type

You are given seven group type options to choose from; alumni, corporate group, conference group, networking group, non profit group, professional group and other.

## Group Summary

When anyone searches for your group your summary will appear in the Groups directory along with your group name and logo. Only about 140 characters of your summary will be displayed so you will need to be brief and to the point and need to include, the purpose of the group, the name of your target audience and the benefits of joining the group.

## Description

Your description is featured on your group profile page which can be accessed by clicking on the 'i' on the top left of your group. You need to make it very clear what the group is for, what the main focus of the group is, and the benefits your group is going to offer your members when they join. Including keywords from your niche will also help you to be found within search, this is also a good place to display your group rules.

## Website URL

One of your main goals for creating a group is going be to generate leads. LinkedIn groups offer you, as a group owner, the perfect opportunity to build your opt-in list and capture leads with a view to converting your group members into customers. To do this you will need to create a landing page for your group with an offer to tempt members to join your opt-in. You can also use this landing page as your group website and include your blog and any online or offline events you wish to promote.

## Membership

You will then be asked whether you want to offer members '**Auto-Join**' or '**Request to Join**' Asking members to 'Request to Join' can make your group appear more valuable, make it more exclusive and help control spam. However you will need to consider whether you have the resources to administer this. You will also be offered options about whether or not members can invite other members, whether they are allowed to display their logo and whether you want your group to be featured in the group directory.

## Language
Select your language.

## Location
You can select a particular geographic location for your group.

## Twitter announcement.
If you tick this box then your group will be announced on the twitter

account which is linked to your LinkedIn profile.

## Agreement
Read the terms of service and then check the box.

## Create group
You will be offered the option to 'Create an Open Group' or a 'Create a Members-Only Group'. Creating an open group will make your group more visible and easier to promote. Members only groups only allow other members to see the content.

When you have created your group you will automatically be offered the opportunity to send out invitations to your connections and contacts and you can also upload a contact file as well. It is best to skip this section and give yourself some time to familiarise yourself with the group admin panel, learn about the features and possibilities available and add some content before sending out invitations.

## GETTING YOUR GROUP READY TO LAUNCH
When you arrive at your group page you can set up and manage everything about your group in the admin panel under the **'Manage'** tab.

## Creating custom emails
As the group manager or owner you can set up your own custom emails, simply click on'Templates' and you will be offered the following:
- Request to Join message
- Welcome Message
- Decline Message
- Decline and Block Message

## Group Rules
As the owner of your group you can create your own group rules. You can add rules in the **'admin panel'** and they will be displayed under the 'i' tab but it is also a good idea to put them in your description and add them to the welcome email you will send to your new group members.

This way as many people get to see the rules as possible. Many groups are a target for spammers and it is easily visible when a group is badly managed.

It is good practice to first write an introduction about what the group is about, the aims of group, the benefits of the group, why you are creating rules, and also what types of actions and content will be welcomed in your group. Here are some examples of rules you may wish to make:

**No spam, self promotion or direct sales pitches are allowed. Members will be immediately removed from the group if these practices are carried out.**

- **No Off Topic Posts** All posts made must be related to the 'Subject' of the group. Any posts which are not will be deleted.
- **No Spamming** Please do not post solicitations about your product or service. Any post like this will be deleted.
- **Job Posts** Please post job postings under the 'Jobs' tab
- **Politics and Religion** No religious or political discussions are allowed.
- **No Inappropriate Postings and comments** No threatening, abusive, discriminatory or harassing comments.

## Group Settings

In Group settings you can manage your permissions about what your members are allowed and not allowed to post. Here you can manage who can post discussions, polls, jobs and promotions and whether or not you are going to screen discussions posted by others before approving their inclusions.

## Creating niche sub groups

Setting up niche sub groups is a great way to broaden your base and attract new people, however only do this if you have the resources available as it's time consuming enough to run the main group. Sub groups are a great way to offer your members value by giving them the opportunity to promote their product or service and also keeps them from self promoting on the main discussions page.

## MANAGING YOUR GROUP

To build a high quality, active and engaged group you will need to do the following:

### Promote your group

A group is no good without members and you will need to commit to spending time building your group membership to get the momentum going. The next section of this chapter is dedicated to the subject of how to build your group membership.

### Post a weekly discussion

You will need to regularly post discussions in your group to create interest. Your discussions need to be about something on topic and about something that your audience relates to and that will provoke discussion. Discussions that provoke an emotional feeling can be very effective. Joining other groups is a very useful way of finding ideas for discussions and you may find a pattern in what works and what does not.

You can also allow your members to post their blogs if related to the subject. LinkedIn Group Digest emails go out daily or weekly to members depending on the activity of the group. The names of people who have created discussions are included in this email, so you want to make sure your name is turning up in that email as often as possible.

You can further promote your discussions by featuring your discussions as the managers choice. To do this click on the title of the discussion and then click on '**Add to Manager's choice**' underneath the profile picture. You can select up to ten discussions to add to the manager's choice and they can be discussions created by any member depending on whether your group allows its members to post discussions. The manager's choice will displayed at the top of your group page, on the carousel and in the group digest emails.

## Welcome message
Automatically send your members a welcome email and ask them to introduce themselves to encourage engagement.

## Send out a weekly announcement
As a group manager or owner you can send out one announcement to your group per week, to your members who have chosen to receive emails. You can include a subject up to 200 characters and a message of up to 4000 characters with URL's. Sending out weekly announcements to your group is proven to be a great way to boost your lead generation if done correctly. You need to make sure you create an attention grabbing headline and share really useful content and encourage members to sign up to your opt-in by offering them a free ebook, or invite them to attend an online event. Announcements are also automatically posted as a featured discussion within the group so you can comment and add to the discussion. Make sure you send a test one to yourself first which will give you an idea of how it will appear to your audience.

## Post a weekly question
Asking open questions is a great way to create interest and encourage comments and discussion.

## Comment on discussions
Commenting and engaging with group members will show your members you appreciate their input and will make them feel valued and will encourage them to contribute again.

## Create LinkedIn polls
Polls create a quick and easy way for people to engage and create conversation and interest. You need to make sure you create a question that your audience will be passionate about. You can specify up to five answer choices for your poll. Simply click on the poll icon to the right of the activity bar and complete the short form.

### Encourage active users

Make sure you encourage active users by quoting them and drawing attention to them and sharing their content.

### Monitor posts

You will need to monitor posts and discussions for spam and misuse. Your group will lose value if it is left open to spam and self promotion from members.

## PROMOTING YOUR GROUP

### Invite your connections or contacts

To send invitations from within the admin panel simply click on **'Manage'** then **'Send Invitations'** on the left menu. You can also design your own email with your group branding and send it to your contacts. Make sure you outline the benefits of your group and what you will be offering.

### Allow group members to send out invitations

You can allow your members to send out invitations to join your groups by choosing the option **'Allow members to invite others to join this group'** in Group Settings'

### Announce on your personal profile and your company page

Announce your group creation on your company page with an image and share on your personal profile too.

### Promote your group on your blog or website

There is no plugin for this but writing an article about your group with the group logo and a clear invitation to join your group on LinkedIn can be an effective way to promote your group to new members.

### Invite Influential People

Invite the most influential people in your niche to join your group.

### Engage in other groups
By joining other groups and contributing with rich and valuable content you will increase the likelihood of people visiting your profile and joining your group. This is a very powerful way of encouraging people to join your group without being too self promotional.

### Announce your groups on other social media platforms
Your followers on other networks will probably feel honoured to be invited to join your group on LinkedIn. Make sure you post a compelling image.

### Make it part of your connection process
When people send you an invitation to connect, send them a message with an invitation to your LinkedIn group and the benefits of joining your group.

### Add to your email signature
Add your group name, logo and description to your email signature.

### Be a good host
Be a good host by involving yourself in discussions, helping people and managing the group well.

# CHAPTER SEVEN

## *ADVERTISING ON LINKEDIN*

WITH ITS HIGH quality audience made up of professionals, senior executives, entrepreneurs, business owners and decision makers LinkedIn is a powerful platform for advertising and reaching your exact target audience. You can develop highly targeted campaigns and reach professional audiences in particular industries, companies and positions and you can tailor make your adverts to those audiences. LinkedIn also allows you to analyze your results so that you can continually make improvements to your campaigns. When people are using LinkedIn they are of a business mindset, and sales conversions can be higher than on any other social network.

Before launching into your first campaign you will need to define your goals. These could be to increase your reach past your current followers on your company page, to drive traffic to your website or blog or generate leads for conversion. You will also need to work out what your expectations are, and the sort of result you hope to achieve.

To drive a successful campaign you will need to create a customised landing page or a page on your website where your audience can take some kind of action. You may want them to join your opt-in, or complete a form in exchange for some valuable content in the form of an ebook, or maybe you have a special offer you would like audience to take up. Whatever it is you need to make sure you have a plan of action to catch these prospects rather than just sending them to a page where they may continue to another website never to be seen again.

## Creating your campaign

LinkedIn adverts can be found throughout the LinkedIn platform, and up to three text, image or video adverts can be seen on profile pages, home pages, inbox, search results and groups.

To start simply click **'Business Services'** on the top right of your profile and then click **'Advertise'** and then **'Get Started'** on the next page. You can choose to either **'Create an advert'** or **'Sponsor update'** .

## Creating your advert

With a Linkedin advert you can target your audience with either text, an image or a video advert. You can create up to 15 advert variations per campaign so you can test different headlines, descriptions, images and different calls to action and see which ones are the most effective. Before you go ahead and create your adverts, it's a good idea to view adverts on LinkedIn and see which ones catch your eye and grab your attention.

- **Campaign name** The first thing you will need to do is choose your campaign name. Creating a name which relates to the audience you are going to target for this particular campaign will help you when it comes to analysing your results and you will easily be able to pinpoint which campaigns are performing better than others.
- **Select your Media type** You will then be offered the option to choose a basic advert( text and image) or a video advert.
- **Advert Destination** Here you can select whether you want to send your audience to your website or your customised landing page or your company page.
- **Create your headline** You have 25 characters to grab your audiences attention and write a strong, brief and specific headline. This is where you can need to offer something useful to your audience or offer some kind of solution to a common problem your audience may share. It needs to be unique and appeal in some way to the emotions of your audience, sometimes a simple question can work very well.

- **Description** You have 75 characters to compose a message so it needs to be concise, to the point and relevant to the landing page to which you are sending your audience. It's here you need to expand on your headline, add a call to action and give them even more reason to click your advert.

- **Your Image** The maximum size for an image is 50 x 50 pixels and you can either use an image relating to your product or your company logo. The space for the image is very small so your image needs to be a close up shot.

- **Video adverts** Video adverts work exactly the same as text adverts except instead of adding an image you can upload a video. When a user clicks the advert, a 30 second video will play and after the video is complete the user can click through to the URL. Videos allow you to expand on your message and they can inspire, educate and sometimes persuade your audience members more effectively than just an image.

- **Targeting** The next step is to select your target audience and this is where you can utilize the power of LinkedIn and the incredible amount of information they hold about their professional members. You can select your audience by location, company type or company name, job title, school, skills, gender, group and age. As you select your audience the figure on the top right will indicate the number of people you will be targeting. You can get as specific as you like, you can even choose specific company names if you like and LinkedIn will also offer you a pre-selection of categorised companies. Groups are a hugely effective way of targeting your audience because they let you target members through their interests.

- **Campaign Options** Just before you are ready to go live with your adverts you need to choose your campaign options. The great thing about LinkedIn adverts is they are self serve and you are totally in control of your budget. You can turn your campaign on or off whenever you like and increase or decrease your bids depending on your budget. You can choose a daily budget and choose whether you prefer to use CPC ( cost per click ) or CPM ( Cost per 1000 impressions) and LinkedIn will suggest a bid.

- **Lead Collection** Lead collection is a free add on that lets people who have viewed your advert, request contact with you. Members that click on your advert will see a lead collection bar above your website that asks them if they wish you to contact them. You will then get an email that notifies you when you have received the lead and you can subsequently reach out to them with a personal email.

**Measuring the effectiveness of your adverts**

The dashboard will show you the effectiveness of your adverts. You will be able to see the number of impressions, the number of click through rates and the number of clicks. In order to run an effective campaign your click through rate needs to be at least 0.025% and the more relevant your advert is to your audience the higher your click through rate will be.

# CHAPTER EIGHT

## *DAY TO DAY ACTIVITY*

THERE ARE CERTAIN things that you will need to do on a day to day basis to run your campaign on LinkedIn. It is a good idea to allot a specific amount of time and a particular time of the day to do this. Here are some of the things you will need to do:

### Following your customer's LinkedIn

This is important if your customers are business owners themselves. Following their company pages on LinkedIn will go a long way in building relationships. By following you are showing them that you are interested in what they have to say and also helping them to achieve their goals by helping to build their audience.

### Showing your audience you value and respect them

If you value and respect your audience they will most probably love, respect and value your business. Be kind, generous, offer as much help and value as possible, reply to their comments and make it obvious that you value them and are listening to them. Don't be afraid to be yourself rather than a stiff brand with no personality.

Everyone is aiming for likes, shares and comments so if you are helping others out by commenting and liking their content it is going to draw attention to your brand and they are more likely to take interest in your content. This is one area where the reciprocation rule works very well on LinkedIn. Engaging with content will also draw attention to you and your brand and you will find that people will click on your name to find out who you are and may want to connect with you. Be friendly to your audience, be chatty, authentic, genuine and embrace the conversation. All this will all go a long well in building a positive image for your brand and will set you apart from your others who are continually ambushing their audience with self promotion.

## Following influencers in your niche

Building relationships with key influencers in your niche is invaluable. Not only can you learn from their content but also these people can have literally thousands of followers, imagine if they follow you back and then share your content!

## Dealing with negative comments

Every business at some time will have to deal with negativity from followers. Hopefully if you have a good product then this is not going to happen too often.

You need to deal with complaints as quickly as possible and be as transparent and authentic as possible. The best thing to do is to apologise and say how sorry you are to hear of the inconvenience they have been caused and offer to continue the conversation and deal with their concern by either private message or telephone. You can then deal with this privately, give your customer the full attention they deserve and decide on your next course of action or compensation.

# CHAPTER NINE

## MEASURING AND MONITORING YOUR RESULTS ON LINKEDIN

MEASURING AND MONITORING your results and performance against your original goals and objectives on a continual basis is essential. This is where many businesses go wrong, they carry on aimlessly posting content without checking to see what is working and what is not. Then after 6 months or a year they wonder why their campaign is making no positive difference at all.

When you measure your results you will discover so much information about your campaign which will allow you to steer your campaign in the right direction to achieve those SMART goals and objectives and stop anything that is not working.

When you originally work out your strategies and tactics for your campaign you will be estimating what you need to do to achieve your goals and objectives. However as your campaign runs you will see exactly what you need to do to achieve what you originally set out to do. For example, you may need to increase the amount you spend on advertising to attract new followers, or you may need to change the types of posts you make to increase engagement and reach. Perhaps you need to increase the number of competitions you run to increase the number of opt-in subscribers. This is what it is all about, making your campaign work for you by constantly measuring your success against the goals set and then adjusting your strategies accordingly in order to achieve the results.

## LINKEDIN ANALYTICS

LinkedIn analytics provides you with metrics and trends for your company page and is split into two sections; Company Updates and Followers.

**Company Updates**

Company updates has three sections; Updates, Reach and Engagement.

**Updates**

Shows a table with the most recent updates as follows:

- **Preview.** This shows the first few words of a post.
- **Date.** The date each update was posted.
- **Audience.** Indicates whether the update was sent to followers or targeted.
- **Sponsored.** Shows which campaign or campaigns you have sponsored an update in.
- **Impressions.** The number of times each update has been shown to LinkedIn members.
- **Clicks.** The number of clicks on your company page, logo or your content.
- **Interactions.** The number of times people have liked, commented or shared an update.
- **Engagement %.** The number of interactions, clicks and followers divided by the number of impressions.
- **Followers acquired.** How many followers you gained by promoting an update.

**Reach**

This displays a graph showing the number of times your updates were seen either organically or through a paid campaign. You can select your preferred date ranges from a drop down menu.

**Engagement**

This displays a graph showing the number of times members clicked,shared or commented your organic or sponsored content.

- **The Followers Section.** The followers section is divided into five sections and show where your followers are coming from.
- **Type.** A daily record of the total number of LinkedIn members

following your page.

- **Organic.** Followers to your page that you gained without advertising.
- **Acquired**. Followers you gained on your page through sponsored updates or company follow adverts.
- **Follower Sources.** The top five places where your followers are coming from as a percentage of your total followers. This could be from search, company page, mobile or paid sources.
- **Follower Demographics.** A breakdown of who is following your company page by seniority, industry, job function and company size.
- **Follower Trends.** This shows how your number of followers has changed over time.
- **How you compare.** This shows you the number of followers compared to other companies.

## GOOGLE ANALYTICS

If you want to look at more detailed information, for example, the number of people LinkedIn is sending to your website or blog or how many of your connections and followers are converting into customers you will need to use Google Analytics. Google Analytics provides advance reports that let you track the effectiveness of your campaign with the following social reports:

**The Overview Report.** This report lets you see at a glance how much conversion value is generated from social channels. It compares all conversions with those resulting from social.

**The Conversions Report.** The conversions report helps you to quantify the value of social and shows conversion rates and the monetary value of conversions that occurred due to referrals from LinkedIn and any of the other social networks. Google Analytics can link visits from LinkedIn with the goals you have chosen and your E-commerce transactions. To do this you will need to configure your goals in Google Analytics which is found under '**Admin**' and then '**Goals**'. Goals in Google Analytics lets you measure how often visitors take or complete a specific action and you can either create goals from the templates offered or create your own custom goals. The Conversions report can be found in the Standard Reporting tab under Traffic Sources > Social > Conversions.

**The Networks Referral Report.** The Networks Referral report tells you how many visitors the social networks have referred to your website and shows you how many page views, visits, the duration of the visits and the average number of pages viewed per visit. From this information you can determine which network referred the highest quality of traffic.

**Data Hub Activity Report.** The Data Hub activity report shows how people are engaging with your site on the social networks. You can see the most recent URL's that were shared, how they were shared and what was said.

**Social Plug-in Report.** The Social Plug-ins report will show you which articles are being shared and from which network. The Google + 1 button is tracked automatically within Google Analytics but additional technical set up is required for LinkedIn, Twitter and Facebook, you can find out how to do this on the Facebook developers site. Other sites like 'AddThis' or 'ShareThis' offer plug-ins as well which automatically report sharing.

**The Social Visitors Flow Report.** This report shows you the initial paths that your visitors took from social sites through to your site and where they exited.

**The Landing Pages Report.** This report shows you engagement metrics for each URL, these include page views, average visit duration and pages viewed per visit.

**The Trackbacks Report**. The Trackback report shows you which sites are linking to your content and how many visits those sites are sending to you. This can help you to work out which sort of content is the most successful so you can create similar and it also helps you to build relationships with those who are constantly linking to your content.

**Tracking custom campaigns with Google Analytics**
Google Analytics lets you create URL's for custom campaigns for website tracking. This helps you to identify which content is the most effective in driving visitors to your website and landing pages. For instance you may want to see which particular updates on LinkedIn are sending you the most traffic or you may want to see which links in an email or particular banners on your website are sending you the most traffic. Custom campaigns let you measure this and see what is and what is not working by letting you add parameters to the end of your URL. You can either add you own or use the URL Builder.

To do this simply type 'URL builder' into Google and click on the first result. The URL builder form will only appear if you are signed into Google. You then need to add the URL, that you want to track, to the form provided and then complete the fields and click 'Submit.' You will then need to shorten the URL with bit.ly or goo.gl/. Once you have set these up you can track the results within Google Analytics.

## OTHER MANAGEMENT TOOLS

**Hootsuite**
Hootsuite is a social media management dashboard that helps you to manage and measure multiple social networks including LinkedIn. You can manage up to five accounts for free and it is designed so you can listen, engage and manage all from one place. Hootsuite is internet based so there is no need to download any software. Other benefits include scheduled tweets and bulk schedule with a csv file and also has built in analytics so you can measure your progress on multiple social networks.

## Buffer

Buffer is an online tool that lets you post to multiple accounts including, LinkedIn, Facebook, Twitter and Google+. Buffer lets you schedule your updates and offers automatic URL shortening and basic analytics. With Buffer you can post on your personal profiles as well as your business pages and also allows you to use bit.ly links so your followers will not know that you are scheduling your tweets. Upgrading allows you to add more accounts and schedule more tweets than the basic free account.

## Socialoomph

Socialooph has an impressive list of features to boost your social media productivity. Not only does it help you manage your LinkedIn, Twitter and Facebook accounts, it also can help you schedule posts to your blog as well. There are free and premium options available.

## CHAPTER TEN

## SLIDESHARE

ANY BOOK ABOUT LinkedIn would not be complete without a section on the incredibly powerful platform SlideShare. SlideShare is the worlds largest community for sharing private and public presentations and helps discover people through content and content through people. LinkedIn acquired the professional content sharing platform in 2012 for approximately 119 million in cash and stocks which demonstrates how valuable SlideShare is for business. SlideShare presentations can be viewed on the website, on hand held devices and they can be embedded on websites as well. Files can be uploaded in the following formats, Keynote, Powerpoint, PDF or OpenOffice presentations and it also supports videos and Webinars.

SlideShare boasts over 60 million visitors a month and its community is predominantly professional and educational which makes it an incredibly powerful platform for B2B's. The most tagged words on SlideShare are business, market, social media, trends and research.

## BENEFITS OF SLIDESHARE

### Features in Google search
SlideShare presentations are very highly ranked in Google's organic search which can offer your business yet another way of being found. All SlideShare presentations are ranked and indexed and information you present on SlideShare is far more likely to be found than on your own site.

## Straight business

People are on this site to have their business questions answered and therefore any presentation that solves their business problem or helps them in some way is going to be valued by the audience, and a business product will be well received by this audience.

## Website traffic & lead generation

SlideShare can boost traffic to your website or blog and can be highly effective in generating new leads. It can also be a great contributor to your sales funnel to drive traffic and build your opt-in list.

## People love images

People do love images and slideshow presentations make learning fun, easy and enjoyable. If you can get your audience to enjoy a learning experience with you, then you are half way there in terms of building a following who may then watch your next presentation.

## SlideShare spreads virally

Since anyone can share or embed a SlideShare presentation they often spread virally through social networks such a LinkedIn, Facebook, Google + and Twitter.

## Connect with new people

SlideShare enables you to upload your ideas and connect with new people who can often help you with new ideas.

## Brand awareness

As with all visual presentations you can publicize and promote your brand by offering relevant and interesting content or answers to questions on topics that your niche are interested in.

## Excellent for the camera shy

SlideShare could be describe as the YouTube of slides. If you are not happy about standing in front of the camera, slides are the next best thing in terms of positioning yourself as a thought leader.

## Cost effective content creation

Creating slide presentations can be a great deal cheaper than video creation particularly if you are not creating your own videos.

## Integration with LinkedIn and Facebook

Both these networks offer integration and LinkedIn will display your most recent presentation on your profile and send out a notification to your network advising them that there is new content.

## SlideShare lead capture

For members who sign up for one of the pro versions of SlideShare there is the ability to activate the user friendly lead capture form. This allows you to obtain information about your followers. You can also incorporate a system where you can grow your opt-in list.

## Measure your success

Through SlideShare analytics you can measure shares on other social media like LinkedIn, Twitter and Facebook. You can find out which pieces of content are giving you the most views and the location of your viewers. You can also see which sites and blogs are giving you the most views.

## Great visibility for your blog

You can upload your blog to SlideShare. If you are new to blogging then this could be a great way to increase the visibility of your blog and get some new followers.

## SETTING UP YOUR PROFILE

To set your profile up for SlideShare it is recommended to set up the free version. You can sign up for pro version later if required where there are some excellent extra marketing features.

Make sure your profile name and picture is consistent with your brand. SlideShare offers you the opportunity to select from eight business types and gives you up to 100 characters for your profile name. This is really useful because you can get really descriptive here and you can include your name and business name and use your personal profile picture which would really help to personalize your brand. It is your profile name that is mostly promoted within SlideShare. You can change your business type and profile name anytime but you can not change your username. For best results your image needs to be square 96 X 96 pixels. You can add a really decent keyword rich 'about' section (up to 700 characters) and you can connect your Twitter, LinkedIn and Facebook profiles which will be displayed under your about section. In the sharing section you are also offered the options to automatically share your presentations with Facebook and LinkedIn.

SlideShare also lets you display your Twitter feed on your profile, simply go to the drop down menu on the top right and Click '**View my profile page**' then on the bottom of this page you can add your Twitter handle and you can choose to display your feed. This is another way to increase you reach and gain followers on Twitter too.

The pro version of SlideShare allows you various levels of branding your profile and you can use preset themes or create your own. The level of investment will be dependent on how much you are going to use the platform.

## TIPS FOR CREATING GREAT PRESENTATIONS

Sharing your slides on SlideShare is going to increase the reach and put your product or service in front of a new audience of business professionals. If you are creating the right content you will be reaching a highly targeted audience of potential customers. If your presentation is good enough you may even get featured on the home page as one of the top presentations of the day. Before you get started it is essential to spend some time checking out as many SlideShare presentations as possible, and this way you can get a feel for what works and what does not. Here are some top tips for creating great presentations on SlideShare:

## Know your goals
Be clear on what your goals are in creating your presentation. If it is generating leads, then it's a good idea to the pro version which will help you capture leads.

## The type of presentations
The best presentation will be about subjects that your audience are interested in and that your audience want to know more about. It could be the answer to a question they need answering. Ask yourself if this is going to add value in some way, is it going to be useful, helpful, or make their life easier in some way? As this is a pretty savvy audience you will need to give them specific answers and high quality information.

## Grab attention with your headline and first slide
- Write a really good attention grabbing headline . Use headlines like
- Top ten tips to …..
- The tip five things……
- The ultimate guide to……
- The complete guide…..
- Five ways to solve…….
- Seven secrets you should know to……….
- Top five ways to make your customers love you.

Your first slide should be highly engaging and visually appealing. By using an extraordinary fact to open your presentation or asking a question like, 'Did you know that………..' is a great way to get your viewers to click the next slide.

## Add a description and tags

Write a compelling description which is keyword rich and add highly relevant tags. It's good idea to include your contact information and any other relevant information.

## Plan your presentation and your slides

Try and sift out what is really important and keep to one message per slide. Storytelling is one of the best ways to gain engagement and keep your audience's attention throughout the presentation to the end.

## Make your slides very visual

People remember images much more easily than text. You can source images from image libraries and also sites like flickr. Make sure you check the image license first before using any images!

## Make sure you include keywords in your slides

SlideShare sources text from slides for search purposes and if you include keywords your presentation is more likely to be found on Google.

## Do not crowd your slides

Adding too much information will only make them look confusing. Whitespace is a good thing! Generally people can only cope with one piece of information at a time.

## Keep a consistent theme

Keep to a few colours and a modern font style. Doing this will make your presentation look far more professional and pleasing to the eye. It is also a good idea to keep your presentation in line with your corporate identity.

## Add Audio or video

Adding narration to your presentation can make it much more personal and engaging. You can now add audio via an app on ipad called 9slides.com . You simply import the presentation and then record audio and video on your ipad and then post it back on the web. Video is under utilized on SlideShare and what many people do not realize is that you are very much more likely to get your video viewed on SlideShare than on YouTube, so make sure you always upload your videos to SlideShare. Creating a talking head video for SlideShare is a great way to start a more personal connection with your followers and viewers.

### Add a call to action

All links on SlideShare presentations are clickable . You could use <u>paywithatweet.com</u> to help share the word about your presentation or direct your viewers to a free offer and opt-in page or ask them to follow you on SlideShare. If you are uploading a video you could ask them to join your YouTube Channel.

## BUILDING YOUR FOLLOWERS ON SLIDESHARE

As with all the social media networks you need to build your targeted audience on SildeShare, here are some tips about how to do this:

### Your Website or Blog

Insert the SlideShare button on your website or blog. You can find the badges and the code to embed in your website or blog <u>http://www.slideshare.net/widgets/minibadge</u>
You can also embed your presentations on your website too, which can also help you to grow your followers. Remember the majority of website traffic disappears into the ether so any way you can catch a website visitor and continue a relationship is good.

### Connect and comment

The more people you connect, the more likely you will be to find new contacts. The first place to start is with your current contacts, it is likely that some of them will already be on SlideShare and if you follow them they will probably follow you back. As soon as you follow a user they will get an email notification and a link so that they can follow you back. Commenting on other peoples presentations is a great way to start conversations as well as exposing your account to others who have commented on a presentation.

## Advertising

Driving traffic through an Adwords campaign to one of your presentations is a great way to generate and capture leads. You can either include your own call to action at the end of the presentation or embed a SlideShare generation form in the middle or at the end of your presentation.

## Share share share

As discussed earlier you can choose to automatically share your presentations with Facebook and Twitter. It is also advisable to share with your other networks like Pinterest. You can also embed your presentation in your linkedIn profile and you can even convert your SlideShow to video and upload it on YouTube for your community there.

## Send email to your contacts

You could also advise your contacts by email that you have a profile on SlideShare and direct them to your presentation.

# LEAD CAPTURE

As mentioned earlier one huge benefit of SlideShare is that you can actually capture leads and view and download them as a csv. To do this you will need to sign up to the Pro version. You then need to select the pro dashboard and then under the word **Capture** select the words **Turn on.**

When the lead capture is turned on visitors will have the option to submit their information on an easy to complete form which then allows them to receive more information about your products. You will need to give your form a title and a message, so you need to be clear about what your goal is before you do this. The fewer questions you ask the more likely your viewer is to complete the form.

## Chapter Eleven

### *Building your Brand with LinkedIn*

YOUR MAIN AIM through this whole process is going to be to connect, capture, and convert your prospects through your website or blog, LinkedIn, and through other social networks, and this involves the following:

- **Connect:** Your product needs to be the connection between your prospect and what they need so the first thing you need to do is connect those two things. In order to do this you need to identify who they are, find them out of all the millions of people on the Internet, and then connect with them by offering them something they want or need.
- **Capture:** Once you have found them you need to capture them on your website, blog, LinkedIn, or any other social media platforms. This is so you can continue your relationship with them either by email or through LinkedIn and communicate your brand message. To do this you need to offer them some sort of incentive so you can capture their name and email address.
- **Convert:** When you have captured your prospect you need to convert them into a paying customer by nurturing them and continuing to build a relationship by offering them the content they want through email and LinkedIn and then moving them toward signing up for a special or exclusive offer.

To achieve this successfully you are going to need to have a well-defined brand, and that brand needs to be communicated through everything you do or say through LinkedIn, your website, blog, and your email campaign.

Whether you are a one person small business, a large corporation, or an organization, your brand is one of the most important attributes of your business. Your brand is what you want your prospects and customers to respect, trust, and fall in love with so they will buy and continue to buy your products and services. Your brand is what is going to set you apart from any other business and what will give your business the competitive edge.

Never has there been a better time for your business to build your brand and communicate your brand message to your target audience than through LinkedIn. Your brand is the main ingredient for success, and LinkedIn is giving you the channel to communicate it. You can literally communicate with your audience every day. If you get it right and connect the right brand experience with the right target audience, you are onto an all-around winner.

It may be that you have a well-established brand already or maybe you have not created your brand yet or it just needs some tweaking or fine tuning. Maybe you are not exactly sure what your brand is, or you feel it needs a complete overhaul. Whatever your situation is, you need to know that your brand is going to underpin your whole LinkedIn campaign, and it needs to be strong, clear, well-defined, and consistent. Once defined, your business is going to create it, be it, communicate it, display it, picture it, speak it, promote it, and most of all, be true to it. This chapter is going to take you through everything you need know and do to define and create your brand so you can get into the hearts and minds of your target audience by communicating the right message and brand experience.

There are many definitions of the word brand but this is the one I like best because it incorporates pretty much all the necessary information you will need to help you to define your own brand.

## Brand, the definition

Your brand is more than a name, symbol, or logo. It is your commitment and your promise to your customer. Your brand is the defined personality of either yourself as an individual brand or your product, service, company, or organization. It's what sets you apart and differentiates your business from your competition and any other business. Your brand is created and influenced by your vision and everything you stand for, including people, visuals, culture, style, perception, words, messages, PR, opinions, news media, and, especially, social media.

## Why is your brand so important to your business?

Branding is important because it helps you and your business build and create powerful and lasting relationships by communicating everything you want to say about your product or service to your prospects and customers. A strong brand encourages loyalty and will ultimately create a strong customer base and increase your sales by doing the following:

- Demonstrating to your prospects and customers that you are professional and committed to offering them what you promise
- Making your business easily recognizable
- Creating a clear distinction from your competition
- Making your business memorable
- Creating an emotional attachment with your audience
- Helping to create trust
- Helping to build customer loyalty and repeat custom
- Creating a valuable asset which will be financially beneficial if you sell your business
- Creating a competitive advantage

To do all the above you are going to have to find a way to get into the hearts and minds of your customers so they will ultimately buy and continue to buy your products or services. Before launching your campaign and setting up profiles, posting content, and engaging, you will need to have a clear picture of exactly what your brand is or what you want your brand to be. You will need to define exactly how your brand is perceived now, how you want your brand to be perceived, where your business fits into the market, who your target audience is, and how you want your business to develop in the future.

To do this you need a deep understanding of your business and the people who are going to be most interested in your products and how you are going to serve them. When it comes to defining your ideal target audience, you need to work out which of your products are the most popular and the most profitable so you can focus your efforts in finding and connecting with the right audience and then creating the right brand experience for them.

## YOUR VISION/ YOUR STORY

If you want to create a strong brand, one of the first things you need to do is create a clear visual picture of how you see your business now and in the future. This is about daring to see what your business could be without constraints or limitations.

This exercise will not only help you work out what you want to achieve financially and creatively, but it also makes you focus on what really matters and will help you create your own unique voice and story. This is incredibly important when it comes to your branding as this is what is going to make your business stand out from others and give you that edge.

To do this, you need to get away from all distractions and think about how you would like to see your business grow and develop in the next three years. This is more than just putting a mission statement together. This is about your core business beliefs, why you are doing it, what you want your business to be, and how you want to be perceived in your market. To help you do this you will need to ask yourself the following questions and record your answers:

- Why did you originally start your business or why are you starting a business?

- How did your original business idea come about?
- What changes are you looking to make in peoples' lives?
- What are you hoping to achieve?
- What aspects of your business are really important to you?
- What are your hopes and dreams?
- What is your definition of success?
- What sort of turnover and income defines that success?
- How many employees does your business have?
- Why are you in business?
- What are your core values in your business?
- What impact do you want to have?
- What influence do you want to have?
- What sort of things do you want the media to be saying about you?
- What do you want your customers to be saying about you?
- How you want to be portrayed on social media?
- How many LinkedIn followers do you want?
- What markets are you in? Are you local, national, or international?

Once you have completed this exercise, you will have all the material you need so that you can create the unique experience required to make your business stand out from all the others in your niche. This is the first step toward creating a brand for your business. This is the beginning of your story.

## DEFINING YOUR BRAND

Whether you are responsible for defining, creating, and developing your brand in-house or you are employing a local branding and marketing agency, you will need to carry out an analysis of your business to define your brand. Completing the following exercise will help you define and clarify your brand:

- A factual description of what your business is and the purpose of your business
- Describe your product or service in one sentence

- List all your products and/or services.
- What are the benefits and features of all of your products?
- Which are your most profitable products/services?
- Which are your most popular products/services?
- Who are your ideal customers for each of your products or services? (Consumer or business, age, gender, income, occupation, education, stage in family life cycle.)
- Out of these customers, which ones who are most likely to buy your most profitable products?
- Is the market and demand large enough to provide you with the number of customers you need to buy your most profitable products and achieve your financial goals?
- If your answer to the previous question is no then ask yourself the same question for each of your other products.
- Who are your three main competitors? (Have a look at their social media profiles)
- What distinguishes your business from your competition? What special thing are you bringing to the market that is of real value? What is your unique selling point? What solutions are your products offering your customers that will meet their needs or solve their problems?
- If you are already in business, write down what your customers are already saying about your business. What do you think they would say about how your product or service makes them feel emotionally? (You may need to ask your customers if you do not already know.) What qualities and words would you use to describe the personality of your business as it is now? Here are some examples of words you may wish to use: high cost, low cost, high quality, value for money, expensive, cheap, excellent customer service, friendly, professional, happy, serious, innovative, eccentric, quiet, loud, beautiful, relaxing, motivating, sincere, adventurous, amusing, charming, decisive, kind, imaginative, proactive, intuitive, loving, trustworthy, extrovert, vibrant, transparent, intelligent, creative, dynamic, resourceful.

- Now, whether you are already in business or starting out, write down all the words to describe how you want and need your brand to be perceived and what qualities you want to be associated with your brand in order to match the needs and expectations of your ideal customers. If you are already in business, hopefully this will be exactly the same as how you perceive you are at the current time.
- What is the evidence that backs up what you have said about your brand? This could be customer testimonials or any evidence about product or service quality.
- What is the biggest opportunity for your business right now?
- What products are you thinking of introducing in the near future?

## How to get into the Hearts and Minds of Your Target Audience

Your target audience is your most important commodity, as they are the future customers and ambassadors of your business. Every single one of them is valuable, and every single one of them can make a difference to your business. This can be because they are actually going to buy your products or simply spread the word by interacting with you on LinkedIn.

However, it's a big social world out there. The possibilities of finding new people are limitless, but targeting everyone is not the solution. The biggest mistake you can make is trying to reach everyone and then not appealing to anyone. Your first step is to identify exactly who the people are who are going to be interested in your products or services, and then you need to find out everything about them. You need to get inside their heads and work out what motivates these people, what their needs, hopes, aspirations, fears, and dreams are. Your product or service is the link between them and what they want. When you know this you can tailor every single message or piece of content toward them.

When you know exactly who your ideal customers are, LinkedIn offers you the opportunity to go find and reach them. It's then up to you to capture them so you can continue to communicate. When you know everything about your customers you are more likely to speak the right language to be able to communicate with them and build trust to the point where the next natural progression is for them to buy your product.

It's only when you truly understand your audience that you can start converting them into customers. Once you know you are targeting the right audience, you can confidently focus every ounce of your effort creating exactly the right content, nurturing them, engaging with them, and looking after them. It's only a matter of time before they will buy your product.

## Creating your ideal customer persona or avatar

The following exercise is absolutely essential. Your answers to the questions will be the very information that is going to help you communicate with your customer in the right way, by providing them with the right content and the correct brand experience. Once you have done this exercise you are going to own some very powerful information. If you do not do this exercise it is very unlikely that you are going to be able to truly connect with your target audience in the way that is necessary to build trust so that you can ultimately convert them into your customers.

Your answers to the questions in the previous section will have given you a clear idea of which types of customers you need to target to give you the best chance of achieving your financial goals. You now need to find out everything about them so you can get your brand into their hearts and minds. The best way to do this is to create an imaginary persona or avatar of your ideal customer and you can build this picture by finding out the following:

- Describe your ideal customer and include the following details: are they a consumer or in business, their age, gender, income, occupation, education, and stage in family life cycle.

- Where do they live?
- What do they want most of all?
- What are their core values?
- What is their preferred lifestyle?
- What do they do on a day-to-day basis?
- What are their hopes and aspirations?
- What important truth matters to them?
- What motivates and inspires them?
- What sort of routines do they have?
- What are their day-to-day priorities?
- How do they have fun?
- What do they do in their spare time?
- What subjects are they interested in?
- Which books do they read?
- Which TV programs do they watch?
- What magazines do they read?
- Who do they follow on social media?
- Who are their role models?
- What really makes them tick?
- What are their fears and frustrations?
- What are their suspicions?
- What are their insecurities?
- What are their typical worries?
- What is the perfect solution to their worries?
- What are their dreams?
- What do they need to make them feel happy and fulfilled?

## Big Questions

To answer the following questions you will need to step inside your ideal customer's mind and imagine you are them.

- How do you feel when you find your product or service? What is your initial emotional reaction?
- What are the words that go through your head?
- How can I justify buying this product for myself?

- Are you ready to buy immediately?
- Do you have any suspicions that the product may not be what it says?
- What are those suspicions? Why do you have them?
- Do you need more convincing?
- What do you need to convince you that the product is right for you?
- What do you feel when you have the product in your hand?

The reason why these are such big questions is because your answers to them will establish whether or not you have correctly defined your ideal customer and whether you have really understood their needs, desires, and fears. If you are imagining yourself as your ideal customer and you are saying "woo-hoo", ecstatically jumping up and down with glee, immediately buying the product, or relieved that you have at long last found the solution to your problem, then you have created the right avatar. If not, then you need to think again.

It's only when you have imagined yourself in the hearts and minds of your target audience that you are going to be able to connect with them on any emotional level. With the information from the above exercise, you will have everything you need to produce exactly the right content to match the needs, desires, and expectations of your ideal customer so that you can create the right brand experience and sell your products. This information is like gold.

## COMMUNICATING YOUR BRAND

Once you have gone through all the processes outlined in this chapter you will have a clear idea about what your brand is, what is stands for, and how you stand out from similar businesses. You now have to work out how to best communicate this to your ideal customer so that when they hear or see your brand name they immediately make that essential emotional connection. This is what is going to make them eventually love your brand above all others.

When you are clear about what your brand is, what it stands for, and how you are going to stand out from other similar businesses, you then need to work out how you can communicate this message in the best possible way. Your main aim here is to create an emotional connection with your target audience that is going to help them grow to love your brand, remember your brand, and remain loyal to it. To do this you need to communicate your brand story through every aspect of your business, including your social media campaign.

With the information you now have you are armed with everything you need to create a consistent brand. If you have not already done so, you can either hand all this information over to a marketing agency or use it yourself to create all the following:

- **Your logo:** Your logo will give a clear guideline for all your promotional material, including your website or blog, stationery, templates, or any marketing material that needs to be created for online or offline promotion.
- **Your brand message: This is** the main message you want to communicate about your brand.
- **Your tagline:** A short, memorable statement about your brand that captures the personality of your brand and communicates how you or your product will benefit your customer.
- **All your 'about' descriptions:** You can communicate your brand story through all your 'about' sections on all your social media platforms you are using.
- **The content you create for your business:** Every piece of content you create for your business needs to be tailor-made for your target audience. You will need to pick who and what subjects or topics you want to be associated with your brand, as anything you pick to write about will be a representation of your brand.
- **Your website and/or blog:** The 'about' page of your website is probably the most visited page on any website and there is a

reason for this. People want to find out about your business and what is different or special about it. This is a great place to introduce and expand on the story of your brand. This is where you can really go to town and communicate your beliefs and uniqueness.. Also, the visual style of your website or blog and your individual voice should be evident throughout your site and be consistent with your brand.

- **Video content:** Videos are an incredibly powerful way of creating a personal connection with your audience. Make sure that whatever video content you produce and whatever you say is always consistent with your brand.

## Chapter Twelve

### *The Essential LinkedIn Marketing Plan*

BEFORE LAUNCHING INTO your campaign you will need to know exactly what you want your business to achieve and what achieve and what you hope to gain through marketing on LinkedIn. Without the necessary planning and preparation, your campaign is very unlikely to succeed.

The next few chapters take you through everything you need to do to plan your campaign before actually posting content. In this chapter you will learn how to create your mission statement, set goals and objectives, and plan the strategies and tactics you need to implement to achieve those goals. In the following chapter you will learn exactly how to prepare your business, your website and blog, and your email campaign so you can capture and convert customers.

### *Creating your Mission Statement*

Many campaigns fail at the first hurdle simply because they do not have a clear idea about why they are undertaking a campaign or what they want to achieve. They set up a LinkedIn profile and have little or no idea why exactly they are doing it. "Everyone else is doing it … we probably should too." Then they launch in without first articulating the purpose of their LinkedIn campaign and aimlessly start posting content. Before long, they realize that this is having no positive effect on their business, and they either give up or continue half-heartedly.

Once you have defined your brand and your target audience you will need to produce your mission statement for your social media campaign. Your mission statement is vital for your business as a whole and for your prospects and customers, and it should clearly state your commitment and promise to them as well as communicate your brand message. You will be able to include this in your LinkedIn profile and on your company page. To create your mission statement, simply follow these for four easy steps:

- **Describe what your business does:** Describe exactly what you do, what you offer, and the purpose of your business.
- **Describe the way you operate:** Include your core values, your level of customer service, and your commitment to your customers. You can include how your core values contribute to the quality of your product or service.
- **Who are you doing it for?:** Who are your customers? Business owners, entrepreneurs, working women, gardeners, shop owners, etc.
- **The value you are bringing:** What benefit are you offering your customers ? What value are you bringing them?

Once you have created your statement, everyone will know exactly what you are about. You will know what you need to deliver to your customers. Your employees will know what is expected of them. Your customers and prospects will know what your promise is and what they can expect when buying your products and services.

## SETTING YOUR GOALS AND OBJECTIVES

Setting goals and objectives is the key to your success on LinkedIn. Once they are set you will be ready to plan and create the strategies and tactics to achieve those goals and objectives and you will be able to review and measure the success of your campaign.

### Definition of a goal

A goal is a statement rooted in your business's mission and it will define what you want to accomplish and offer a broad direction for your business to follow. The three main goals of any business will ultimately be to increase sales, to reduce costs and to improve customer service and each goal will have a direct effect on the others. Here are some examples of goals and objectives within those three main goals:

## 1. To Increase revenue and generate sales
- To increase website traffic.
- To increase brand awareness through LinkedIn
- To build a reputation as an expert within the industry.
- To build a loyal and engaged community on LinkedIn.
- To increase the number of customers from word of mouth and referrals.
- To increase the number of sales.
- To increase average spend per customer.
- To increase the number of leads generated.
- To introduce new products.
- To increase online visibility.
- To promote an event.
- To build a highly targeted list of email subscribers.
- To connect with new customers.
- To build trust and build relationships with prospects and customers.
- To put a content marketing strategy in place.
- To increase business in 'X' country/state.
- To become a thought leader in your industry.
- To develop new markets by introducing your products into 'X' country/state.
- To decrease spend on traditional forms of advertising and invest 'X' amount in LinkedIn marketing.
- To build relationships with key influencers on LinkedIn.

## 2. To reduce Costs
- To decrease spend on traditional forms of advertising and invest in LinkedIn marketing.

## 3. To deliver customer satisfaction and retain customers
- To answer customer questions promptly.

- To respond to customer complaints promptly, politely and helpfully.
- To provide online help/technical support.
- To respond to customer feedback.
- To listen to your customers.

## Setting measurable objectives

Once you set your broader goals then you need to get more specific and create SMART objectives (specific, measurable, attainable, relevant and time bound). Here is an explanation of exactly what each of those terms means:

- **Specific** You need to target particular areas for improvement.
- **Measurable** Your progress needs to be quantifiable and putting concrete figures on your goals is essential for success and is the only way to measure the effectiveness of your campaign.
- **Attainable / Realistic** You need to be realistic with the resources you have available and the results you are expecting need to be realistic.
- **Relevant** Your goals need to be relevant to the business climate you are in.
- **Time Bound** Make sure you set a realistic time period to achieve your goals. If a time is not set then things don't tend to get done.

Here are some examples of the sort of SMART objectives you should be setting:

- Increase sales of product X by X%
- To build an audience of X number followers on LinkedIn company page within one year.
- To increase number of followers by X per week.
- To increase website traffic from LinkedIn by X times.
- To increase opt-in list subscribers by X per week
- Increase conversions from LinkedIn by X per week.
- To increase the number of leads generated from LinkedIn by X per week.
- To increase the number of new customers by X per month.
- To increase the average spend per customer by X.

- Introduce X number of new products every 6 months.
- To decrease spend on traditional forms of advertising by X and invest X amount in LinkedIn advertising.
- Utilize LinkedIn to increase attendants at X event by X people.
- Utilize LinkedIn to increase YouTube views by X people per week.

## CHOOSING YOUR STRATEGIES AND TACTICS

Once you have set your quantifiable goals and objectives you are going to have to work out how you are going to accomplish them using LinkedIn. You will need to think about the strategies and tactics you are going to use and they need to be quantifiable as well. Here are some examples of the strategies you may want to implement:

- To post 'X' number of updates on personal profile per day.
- To increase connections by 'X' number per week.
- To create a like gate with built in subscriber opt-in form.
- To post content on Linkedin company page 'X' times per week.
- To send 'X' number of InMails per week to new contacts.
- To endorse skills for 'X' number of connections per week.
- To Join 'X' number of groups.
- To create a LinkedIn group.
- To post 'X'number of discussions per week in LinkedIn Group
- To post 'X' number of discussions per week in Groups.
- To spend 'X' minutes participating in Groups per week.
- To spend 'X' amount on LinkedIn advertising.
- To create 'X' number of blog posts per week/month and post them on LinkedIn with images.
- To post 'X' number of offers per month/6 months on LinkedIn.
- To run 'X' number of competitions/contests per year on LinkedIn.
- To create 'X' number of blog posts per month and post details on LinkedIn.
- To create 'X' number of videos on YouTube per month.
- To spend 'X' minutes per day liking customers pages (B2B only.)

- To spend 'X' minutes per day liking, commenting and sharing customer posts.
- To follow 'X' number of influencers on LinkedIn per week.
- To create 'X' number of online events per year.

Of course at the beginning you are going to need to make an educated guess at the number of times you are going to need to do one thing to achieve another. As your campaign runs you will need to adjust certain aspects to achieve what you set out to achieve. For example, you may need to send out more InMails in order to increase your connections or you may need to change the type of content you are posting to increase the amount of engagement. The only way you can do this is by constantly monitoring and measuring your results against the original goals and objectives you set and adjusting your campaign accordingly.

## CREATING YOUR LINKEDIN POSTING CALENDAR

Now that you have your strategies in place, you will have a good idea of the amount and type of content you need to post to achieve those objectives. One of the most challenging tasks of your LinkedIn campaign is going to be to consistently deliver a high standard of content to your fans on a daily basis. You are going to need to post between one to four times a day. This does not mean you need to create numerous blog articles each day, but you are going to need to communicate in some way and find unique ways for your audience to interact with your brand and offer some kind of value on a regular basis. This may seem daunting to begin with, but you will be surprised just how one idea leads to another.

To help you map out your content for the next six months or the year ahead, you need to create a LinkedIn posting calendar which is going to be your key to consistent posting. There are many online tools and apps that can help you with this. Google Calendar is a very good calendar to use, and it lets you color code the different types of posts. You can also use Hootsuite, the social media dashboard, to plot out your calendar or use a spreadsheet in Excel. There are also other online applications, like www.trello.com, which has easy to use drag-and-drop features. Using mind-mapping applications like 'Simplemind' can really help when brainstorming for content ideas.

To get started you will simply need to map out and schedule the days of the week for each week of the year and decide what types of post you are going to create for certain days. You will need to balance the type of content in order to create variety and interest for your audience. You then need to create topics or themes and break the year down into weeks/months and make a schedule. You can add all the things that you are planning within your business, like offers, contests, product launches, and webinars, and then add all the things going on outside your business, like public holidays and special events. You need to incorporate all that information into your daily action plan.

It may seem daunting to look at a blank calendar, but you will be surprised how it comes together when you start breaking it down into months, weeks, and days. A posting calendar will help you keep your campaign focused, on track, and in line with your brand and your marketing goals and also keep it balanced in terms of the subject and type of media you use. A calendar will help you look ahead and help you to incorporate your marketing plan into your LinkedIn campaign. It may be that you are launching a new product, or maybe certain products tie in with specific holidays. You may have certain industry events you need to attend or are perhaps creating your own. Maybe you are going to run a competition at a certain time of the year. Whatever it is you are planning throughout the year, you need to include it on your calendar.

The following example shows how by creating a regular weekly schedule you can really simplify the process of creating your social media posting calendar:

**Week 1**
**Monday**
**AM**          Inspirational quote image to start the week.

**PM**          Post a useful tip.

**Special**     Post Competition teaser.

## Tuesday

**AM**          Link to weekly blog post with image.

**PM**          Post a SlideShare presentation.

## Wednesday

**AM**          Link to educational YouTube video.

**PM**          Fill in the blank post.

## Thursday

**AM**          Post an engaging question which is business related (B2B)

**PM**          Post or share an Infographic (B2B)

**Special**     Post contest photo and entry details.

## Friday

**AM**          Share a business tip (B2B)

**PM**          Post a weekend photo wishing all a happy weekend.

**Special**     Holiday Weekend Post.

## Saturday

**AM**          Post a question that is not business related.

## Sunday

**AM**          Share a funny video.

**PM**          Post a relaxing image for a Sunday.

This is just an example and you obviously need to tailor make this to your business with the content that is important to your particular target audience.

# CHAPTER THIRTEEN

## *PREPARING YOUR BUSINESS FOR SUCCESS*

WHETHER YOUR SITE is being found through an organic search, an advertising campaign, LinkedIn, or any other social media platform, all your hard work is going to be wasted unless you have put a system in place to capture leads and convert them into customers. This system has to start from the moment your prospect either hits your website, your blog, or your LinkedIn page, and your ultimate goal is to convert your browsers into buyers.

Firstly, the unfortunate fact is that the majority of your website visitors are unlikely to buy from you on their first visit. If you do not have a website that grabs their attention within the first couple of seconds, they will move very quickly onto another site. Secondly, even if your site does catch their eye, they are still likely to check out other sites and still may not return. To make any kind of impact at all your site needs to grab their attention and then capture their email address so you can continue your relationship with them through email. This chapter is going to take you through steps you will need to take, from getting your website or blog ready to setting up and creating your email campaign.

Email is still one of the most powerful ways to convert prospects into customers and has a conversion rate three times higher than social media conversion rates. That is not to say that your LinkedIn campaign is any less important, as this is where you are going to find and nurture your leads and transfer them to your opt-in by either capturing them on LinkedIn or on your website or blog. This chapter is going to take you through steps you will need to take from getting your website or blog ready to setting up and creating your email campaign.

## *Preparing your Website for Success*

Whether you already have a website or blog or you are creating a new site from scratch, you need to make sure it has the necessary features to grab the attention of your target audience and capture their email addresses. Capturing the email addresses of your target audience has to be one of your most important goals when creating your website. Once your prospects have voluntarily submitted their email address, you have the opportunity to build a relationship, communicate your message, and promote your products and services on an ongoing and regular basis. A well thought-out and crafted email campaign can immediately establish trust and favor with your subscribers. Don't forget that it is you who owns your opt-in list and nobody can take it away from you. As long as you are providing your subscribers value with great content, they are likely to want to keep hearing from you. Remember you cannot rely on social media to continue your relationship as these platforms are changing all the time. You need to build your email list.

Once you have completed the exercise in the branding section and have your ideal customer persona or avatar, you will have a clear picture of what your target audience's pain point or problem is and how your product can help solve it or make their life better in some way. If you have a blog, and most businesses today need a blog, you will also have all the tools you need to create the right content to attract your target audience. Armed with this information you are halfway ready to putting a system in place, so your products sell themselves and your website is working like an extra sales person selling your products 24/7.

When your visitor arrives at your site, you have only three seconds to grab their attention. You need to connect emotionally with them and let them know immediately that they have arrived at the right place by communicating exactly how you are going to help them and what it is you are offering them.

Once they are on your site, you then need to win their interest and confidence so that they will voluntarily submit their email address. To do this you will need to create a lead magnet and offer your audience something which is incredibly valuable to them for free. There are numerous ways you can do this and which one you use will depend very much on what type of business you are and what your goals are. If you are a business offering technical solutions, you could offer them a free trial. If you are offering information, you could offer them a free report, a short video training series, or an ebook. If you are selling some kind of product or service, you could offer them a money-off voucher. These work particularly well for restaurants and the service industry as a whole. Whatever you are offering, it needs to be really good to attract your audience and get them to volunteer their email.

Here are the features you need to have on your website or blog or any landing page with a special offer.

- **Keep your design simple:** Your site needs to have a clean and simple design, and you need to communicate your most important message clearly and concisely to your target audience. Your most important content with any call-to-action needs to be placed above the fold, where they will be easily seen, and your call-to-action should have an easily seen button link rather than just a text link.
- **Make your site easy to navigate:** Really this is so important. Try to use the minimum number of pages you can and make your menu titles as easy to understand as possible.
- **Clearly communicate your message:** You want your visitors to subscribe to your opt-in, so you need to place your compelling offer with an image and title of the offer someplace where it is visible. The message and benefit of your offer needs be descriptive and specific.
- **Add a clear call-to-action:** In order for your visitors to sign up,

they will need to be told what to do. Make sure you have a direct call-to-action, for example, "Download your free ebook now" or "Sign up for your discount voucher now." Your call-to-action needs to be clearly visible with an eye-catching button link which is much more effective than a text link.

- **Add clear contact information:** Make it easy for your prospects to contact you by placing your contact details where they will be easily seen. With the technology available, you can even add chat features so that as soon as your prospect arrives on your site a chat form appears asking if you can be of any assistance. Obviously you need the resources to be able to man this, but it is an incredibly powerful way of quickly building trust and showing how much you value your website visitors by being available to answer any of their questions.

- **Email capture form:** Your email capture form needs to be as simple as possible, preferably just asking for their name and email. You need to state on the form that their email address is safe with you and will not be shared with anyone. Make sure your form is in a prominent position and consider using a pop-up form that appears 20 seconds after your prospect has arrived on your site. Your email sign-up form needs to go at the top, side, and bottom of your webpage and also on your 'about page,' which is often the most popular page on your site.

- **Privacy policy:** You need a clear privacy policy on your website to make it clear that you will not be spamming them or selling their information.

- **Thank you page:** Once your visitor has completed the form, you will have them as a lead, but before you let them go you can send them to a thank you page where you can offer them the opportunity to share your offer with their friends by including social sharing buttons.

- **Mobile Friendly:** You need to make sure your offer is easily visible and easy to complete on a cellphone. This is incredibly important, as more and more people are purchasing from their cellphone. There is nothing more annoying for the user than if the site is hard to navigate from their cellphone.

- Don't add external links to other sites. Be careful not to fall into the trap of wanting to make your site more interesting by adding lots of content and links to other external sites, as this will only detract from your main goals and you'll end up sending traffic away from your site.

## Landing pages

Landing pages are incredibly effective if you want to promote specific offers for specific products to specific audiences. A landing page is a page that is designed to give information about an offer and then capture a lead with a form for your visitor to complete so that they can download or claim that offer. Landing pages are highly effective in capturing leads because they are designed to be specific in their goal, which is to capture the contact information of your visitor.

The landing page should have a clear, uncluttered design and not have any links or navigation menus that could take your visitor away from the landing page. It should contain the following:

- A headline (The title of the offer)
- A description of the offer, clearly detailing the benefits to your visitor
- A compelling image of the offer
- A clear call-to-action. This can be in the form of an image or text.
- A form to capture contact information (The fewer fields required to be completed, the more leads you will receive.)
- A clear privacy policy on your website that makes it clear that you will not be spamming them or selling their information
- A thank you page leading them to another offer or social sharing

You can either ask your web developer to create landing pages or there are numerous tools available on the Internet where you can easily create one, for example: www.leadpages.net, www.unbounce.com, www.launcheffect.com, and www.instapage.com

## SETTING UP AND CREATING YOUR EMAIL CAMPAIGN

Once you have created your lead capture system on your website, blog, or separate landing page and have your subscribers' permission to send them your email, you are going to need a really good email campaign to convert those leads into sales.

Email is still one of the most effective forms of converting leads into sales, and email is more powerful than ever. Not only is it cost effective but it also provides one of the most direct and personal lines of communication with your customer. Once subscribed, they have invited you into their inbox on a regular basis and producing valuable content for your subscribers will develop trust and deepen your relationship with them. Your email will also work hand in hand with your LinkedIn campaign. As you build your relationship with your connections on LinkedIn, they are more likely to deem your emails valuable and open them.

The first thing you need to do is set yourself up with a good email marketing provider and there are many you can choose from: www.aweber.com, www.constantcontact.com, and www.mailchimp.com to name a few. It's important to use a system where you have a confirmed opt-in. This is when the subscriber is sent an email to confirm their email address. This verifies that you are gaining consent and legally protects you. It also helps you to keep a clean list, and it protects you from sending emails to incorrect addresses. You can then automate your emails with an auto responder and send out emails automatically over time.

Your next task is to plan and create your email campaign. Here are a few tips for doing so:

- **Be clear about your goals:** You need to be absolutely clear from day one what you want to achieve through email. Are you using it to introduce a new product at some time? Are you launching an event? Whatever you do, make sure you know exactly what it is that you want to achieve.

- **Keep it simple and in line with your branding:** Make sure your email design ties in with your branding. Most email providers offer templates which you can add your own branding to, or you can get a designer to create a particular design. Keep it really simple. Sometimes if things are too fancy they become impersonal.

- **Send a regular newsletter:** Plan to send a regular newsletter email at least once a month and once a week if you can. You can also plan to send off information about offers which tie in with special holidays and occasions throughout the year or competitions or events that you may be planning.

- **Plan your topics:** You need to plan the topics you want to cover in each email, and this should tie in nicely with the plan for your blog articles. You then need to deliver high quality content which is tailor-made to fit with your subscribers' interests, and it needs to be so good that they are looking forward to the next email from you. If you are sending emails about offers then you need to show them clearly how these offers are going to benefit their lives.

- **Attention-grabbing titles:** This is where you need to get really creative. Your main goal here is to get your subscriber to open your email, and you need to create a headline that is going to make your subscriber curious and inquisitive and eager to open your mail. Questions work really well as titles, and you will often see your open rates increase. This is because people find questions intriguing and they feel like you are directly addressing them. Try and avoid the words that will trigger spam filters. Simply search Google for a list of these words to avoid.

- **Be authentic and true to your brand:** Write your emails in a style that your audience will grow to recognize, 'like,' and identify with your brand. Write so your subscriber feels like you are just writing to them. You need to establish yourself as a likeable expert for your subscribers. Try and create a personal relationship with them by addressing them by name and giving them a warm friendly introduction. Offering them the opportunity to connect with you and answer any of their questions by simply replying to your mail is a great way to create a connection and trust.

- **Keep it simple** Make sure your emails are simply constructed and straight to the point so you keep your subscribers' interest and get them quickly to the place you want them to go, like your blog or offer.

- **Include social sharing buttons:** Include all your social sharing icons and links in your mail.

- **Make them feel safe:** Make sure your subscribers are clear that their email will not be shared and that they can unsubscribe anytime.

- **Analyze your open rates:** Most email service providers include statistics in their packages so you can analyze open rates, bounce rates, click through rates, unsubscribers, and social sharing statistics. These results give you the opportunity to find out what is and what is not working.

## CHAPTER FOURTEEN

### *BLOG BLOG BLOG*

THIS CHAPTER IS for anyone who does not have a blog. The word blog has been mentioned numerous times throughout the book and has become an essential part of any online business today.

### *WHAT IS A BLOG?*

A blog (short for web log) is a term used to describe a website that provides an ongoing journal of individual news stories which are based around a certain subject or subjects (blog posts). Blogs have given people the power of the media. Anyone can now create a personal type of news that appeals to a high number of small niche audiences.

Bloggers simply complete a simple online form with a title and body and then post it. The blog post then appears at the top of the website as the most recent article. Over time, the posts build up to become a collection, which are then archived chronologically for easy reference. Each blog post can be a discussion with space for comments below the post where readers can leave comments and questions. This is where bloggers start to build relationships and a community with their readers and other bloggers who may have similar interests. Blogs were one of the earliest forms of social media, and they started growing in the late 1990s. The number of blogs has exploded in recent years, and they now underpin the majority of successful social media campaigns.

### *WHY BLOG FOR BUSINESS?*

Blogging is one of the most beneficial tools that a business has to communicate its expertise and ideas to its prospects and customers and to engage with them. Businesses can share information about their business and about any subject that may be of interest to their niche. It is a fact that businesses with blogs benefit from an increase in the number of visitors to their website, increased leads, an increase in inbound links, and increased sales. Here are some of the reasons why and the benefits that come with blogging:

• **Underpins your whole social media campaign:** Your blog is the focus of all your social media efforts and the center of all your content marketing efforts. One of the main goals of any business today will be to get people to their blog to read their valuable and targeted content. Social media will be one of the main tools they can use to drive traffic to their blog.

• **Increased website traffic:** A well-optimized blog will increase your chances of being found in searches. Google loves unique, fresh content, and if this is created regularly, it will boost your traffic.

• **Builds brand awareness**: A blog offers a business the opportunity to build a community and awareness for their products or services. The more people who see your blog, the more people see your brand.

• **Provides valuable information for your niche:** Creating a blog gives your business a voice and provides your niche with valuable information in relation to the subjects they are interested in. This may include information about market trends, industry news, and insight into your products and services and what is behind them.

• **Thought leadership:** Sharing your expertise with valuable information will make you stand out as a thought leader in your particular field and help you build a professional online reputation.

• **Builds trust & creates warm leads:** When you are providing valuable content for your niche on a regular basis, answering their questions, and addressing their concerns, this in turn creates trust between you and your prospective customers. This trust leads to more leads and will result in sales. When your audience becomes regular readers of your blog, they become warm rather than cold leads. The ice has been broken, and they are halfway there in terms of buying your product.

• **You gain more knowledge:** While writing your blog you will be continually researching your subject, learning about new technology, products, and trends. In turn, this keeps you ahead of the game. In the eyes of your customers, it makes you an expert. As time goes by you become more and more knowledgeable and can steer your business in line with market trends and keep your products and services up to the minute. You will also find that blogging is inspiring and your ideas will snowball. As you learn more, you will find more material to blog about.

• **Interaction and feedback:** When your blog has room for comments and discussion it will give you the opportunity to hear what people are saying, the questions they are asking, and insight into what they want out of your products. Feedback like this is invaluable to your business, and it also leads to more ideas for more blog posts. This kind of feedback also encourages a conversation, and you actually get the opportunity to communicate with prospective customers.

## HOW TO CREATE A BLOG

Creating your blog is incredibly straightforward. There are a number of free blogging platforms that are available. However, if you read the terms and conditions of most of these platforms you will find that at the end of the day you do not actually own the content and you will not have full control of your blog. You will have no control of the advertising displayed, you are unlikely to be able to include an email capture form, you will not be able to have you own domain name, and you will not be able to install plugins. With a free platform, your domain name will look something like http://mybusinessblog.theirblogplatformname.com. Overall, it is not going to look that professional.

The best and safest way of creating a blog and running with your own domain name is to create one with wordpress.org or you can use website creators like www.wix.com or www.squarespace.com. Both website creators offer blogs with their product, and you can add your own domain. Using any of these will give you full control over your site.

Wordpress.org is a free open source platform, which means it can be modified and customized by anyone. You can use custom themes or choose from hundreds of free themes and plugins. The wordpress.org blogging platform is free, but you will need to purchase a domain name and host your site on your own server. However, most hosting companies offer inexpensive monthly plans and a one-click installation solution. You will also need to make sure you backup your blog. You may very well find that this is included in your hosting package.

## WHAT MAKES A SUCCESSFUL BLOG

For those businesses that are doing it right, blogging can be hugely beneficial. The company will often see an increase of over 50% of website visitors and leads. However, many blogs also fail to make any positive difference to a business, so it is essential that before you waste time and resources you understand what you need to do to create a successful blog:

### Set Goals and objectives

First of all, you will need to be clear about what your marketing goals are and set clear objectives for what you want to achieve from your blog.

### Example Goal 1

Increase brand awareness through Facebook.
**Objective:**
Achieve X number of shares per month on Facebook.

### Example Goal 2

Increase Traffic to website from blog.
**Objective:**
To achieve an increase of X traffic from blog.

### Example Goal 3

Increase the number of leads for product A.

**Objective:**

To gain X number of new opt-ins per week.

### Example Goal 4

To create interaction and engagement.

**Objective:** To have at least X number of comments on each blog post.

### Example Goal 5

To become a thought leader in the industry.

**Objective:**

To write X number of guest posts per month/year.

### Example Goal 6

To increase the ranking of your blog in Google and Bing.

**Objective:**

To achieve X number of backlinks from other websites in 6 months.

### Create top content for your audience

Again it's all about your audience and what they want, what they are interested in, what makes them tick, and what problems they need solved. If you can identify these things then you are half way to finding the valuable content that is going to keep your audience interested and engaged. When you create your content it needs to be either inspiring, educational, informative, or entertaining. If you can create content that people really value, they are more likely to share your content, sign up for your updates, and come back looking for more. Creating content around your product or services is not going to provide enough interest to your readers and it is unlikely to get shared. Of course the occasional post is okay, but try and keep away from this unless you can tie it in to something which is of real value to your audience.

### Create a content plan

Your content plan is the backbone to your blog. You will need to decide what topics you are going to build your blog around so that you can stay consistent. There may be certain keywords you want to target and need to incorporate into your content. Once you know your topics or subjects, you can decide which types of posts you are going to create. There are numerous types of blog posts you can use, such as tutorials, how to's , interviews, reviews, book reviews, advice, Q and A's, case studies, trend reports, and the latest news in your industry. Once you have decided on all this, you then write a schedule. If you have certain events that happen every year in your industry, make sure you include these in your plan.

## Newsworthy posts

Make sure you are blogging about what's new in your industry. Keep an eye on trending topics related to your industry so you can create blog posts that are really up-to-date. You can do this by checking out what is trending on the social sites and also signing up for Google alerts, which will keep you up-to-date on new info related to your interests and queries.

## Frequent and consistent blogging

It is proven that the more high quality content you produce, the more views your blog will get. You will need to post at least once a week, if not more. Google loves fresh content so the more posts you have, the more opportunities you have to be found.

## Optimize your blog for searches

Look for keywords and phrases that people are looking for. There are tools available to do this, like word tracker, Google trends, and Google keyword planner. You can find out the amount of competition by typing a phrase into Google search and seeing how many results it brings up. In order to get found you will need to concentrate your efforts on low competition keywords and phrases, and the more specific your words and phrases are, the better. You can then create your content around your chosen keyword or phrase, as long as the content is highly relevant. When creating your blog post, make sure you put the word/

phrase in the page title, the header, and the body. If you put the phrase in your meta tag, it will be displayed in bold font in the search results, which will make it stand out even more.

## Attention grabbing headline

To catch your readers' attention, you need a good headline. It should be a headline that will intrigue your audience enough to make them feel that they absolutely have to read this post. It needs to be simple and to the point, as well as contain valuable keywords. Here are some example headlines that really work:

How to .......
7 ways to successfully .........
Why you should do ..... to .......
Secrets that every ...... should know
The secret formula for success in ......
5 quick and easy ways to .........
What every serious ...... should know about......
7 things every ..... should avoid to ......

## A great design

Your blog needs to be inviting, and although the content is what people are looking for, the blog still needs to be visually appealing and reflect your brand. If your blog is just text based, it's going to look cold and uninviting and lack interest, so you need to include compelling images to engage your audience. It is definitely a good idea to spend time researching different themes. Another thing to watch with your design is your side bar. Make sure you have only what is absolutely necessary so you do not pull your readers' attention away from the action you want them to take.

## Formatting

You need to make it as easy as possible for your reader to read and digest your blog. If you format your blog with headings, bold subtitles, and bullet points, it will be much more enjoyable to read than one long paragraph.

### Ask a question at the end of your post

Asking a question at the end of your post is likely to provoke discussion. People like to think their opinions matter, and it's a great way for your readers to interact and network with each other, too. Make sure you answer any questions your readers ask. There is nothing worse than seeing bloggers ignoring their readers.

### Tags

Tags help people find your content within your blog and search engines. They also help group related posts together.

## 11 THINGS EVERY BLOG SHOULD HAVE

### An incentive to join your opt-in

One of the main goals of your blog is to captures leads. The majority of your readers will probably only read one of your blog posts so it's really important to try and get them on your opt-in list so they will keep reading your blog. You will need to make sure you give them some kind of incentive to complete the email capture form, like a free report, free ebook, or simply email updates.

### An engaging image

A blog needs at least one image to make it look interesting and inviting. Blogs without images are simply boring. You can use your own images, stock photos, or images from photo sharing sites like Flickr.

### Clear call-to-actions

You need to make it very clear both within and outside of your text. what you want your readers to do. This could be anything from signing up for email updates, a free trial, a free offer, a request for a quote, or more information on a product.

## Email capture form

You can either include a prominent form on your blog or install a pop-up mail capture form. If you do install a pop-up then make sure the reader has a good few seconds to read the heading and start reading the article before the form pops up. It is also a good practice to put at least three email sign-up forms on the page, one below the article, one in the footer, and one on the top beside the article or right above it.

## About section

Your "about" section is the introduction to you and your blog. It's probably the most viewed page of any blog. People like to know who is writing the blog and feel acquainted with that person, so you need to get your personality over in this section. Make sure you include your name and a picture of yourself. This will help your readers make a personal connection with you. A video of yourself is also a great a way of getting your readers acquainted too. Above all, focus on how you are going to help your readers, what problems you are going to solve for them, and introduce some of the topics you are going to talk about. Remember, your blog is about your audience's needs and not yours.

## Contact page

A simple contact form works best but also make it really easy for people to reach out to you. Make sure you include all your social sharing buttons and an email capture form.

## Easy to search archives

If the content of your blog posts is interesting your readers are going to want to read more so you need to make the previous blog posts easily accessible. On many sites it really is incredibly difficult to find content, so you need to get yourself a custom archive page. A search box at the top of your blog is a great idea for helping your readers find content.

## Social sharing plug-ins

You need to include buttons or links to all the social networks where you have a presence. There are hundreds of plug-ins you can use to do this. Also make sure you have sharing buttons next to your articles as well.

### RSS Feed

RSS (Rich Site Summary) is a format for delivering regularly changing content on the Internet. It saves you from checking the sites you are interested in for new content. Instead, it retrieves the content from sites you are interested in. Make sure you have the RSS feed and then have a clear call-to-action making it clear why they should subscribe to your feed. If you want to keep up-to-date with your favorite bloggers you can sign up to either My Yahoo, www.bloglines.com, or www.newsgator.com.

### Comments section

Your blog needs a comment section which will encourage interaction and help you to build relationships with your readers. You can install Facebook comments easily with a WordPress plug-in. Disqus is another favorite comment provider.

### A guest bloggers welcome page

Guest posting is becoming more and more important in the blogging community and making it obvious that you will accept guest posts is going to go a long way to building relationships with other bloggers. The benefits of having other people contributing to your blog are that you will have more valuable content on your site and more exposure if your guest blogger promotes their posts on their site. You may also gain from the opportunity to produce a guest post on their blog at a later date. Guest blogging is a top method of getting back links to your blog, which is essential for search engine optimization.

### Privacy policy & terms of service pages

Make it clear your email readers are safe with you and you are not going to share their information with any other parties.

## PROMOTING YOUR BLOG

If you want to run a successful blog, you cannot just rely on search to get it out into the blogosphere. You need to find other ways of promoting your content and getting found.

- **Promote on your social sites:** Posting your blog content on social sites is essential. You can connect your blog to Twitter and Facebook so your content is automatically shared. Or you can use Hootsuite or Tweetdec to share your content to multiple sites, which will save you time. When posting, use an image to grab your audience's attention and make sure you use popular hashtags for your topic which will open up more opportunities to being found by new people.

- **Guest blogging:** Guest blogging is a great way of gaining a larger following. It will also give your blog more exposure, credibility, and increase your inbound links, which is essential for SEO. Most bloggers allow guest bloggers to post their bio, including their social profiles and blog URL, on their site.

- **Social sharing buttons:** As mentioned previously, it is essential to have social sharing buttons next to your blog articles.

- **Comment on other blogs:** There is so much opportunity for you to promote yourself today with the number of blogs and social sites. If you comment on other peoples' blogs you can often leave a URL, but only if it is relevant to the article being commented on and you are adding some value to the article.

- **Website and email:** If you have a website then try and point people to your blog. You can do this by adding visual links on your "about" page and other pages. Also make sure you have a link to your blog in your email and send an email to your current contacts telling them about your blog.

- **Create a Google Adwords campaign:** If you are serious about driving traffic to your site and generating leads and you have your blog set up to catch leads and subscribers, an Adwords campaign may kick start your traffic while you are waiting for your blog to get found naturally in search results. Getting quick results like this will also allow you to see if your blog design and format is working and whether any incentives you are offering are enough to generate subscribers and leads.

- **Submit your blog to Reddit and Stumbleupon:** Both of these websites allow their users to rate web content. Reddit is a collection of webpages which have been submitted by its users. Stumbleupon is a collection of web pages that has been given the thumbs up. You can submit pages directly on its submit page or by installing the Firefox add-on or the Chrome extension. It is best not add too many of your own pages to Stumbleupon but make sure you add both the Reddit and Stumbleupon buttons to your blog so other people can.

## THE ESSENTIAL WORDPRESS PLUGINS

One of the best things about WordPress for your blog is that it is easy to customize and you need little or no technical or design knowledge to create a great blog. There are a ton of plug-ins you can install to make your site even better, but there are so many it is difficult to choose which ones are really important. To help you, here are some plug-ins that are essential for your blog:

- **The Facebook comments plug-in:** Installing Facebook comments into your blog can be tricky, but with this easy to use plug-in you can easily administer and customize Facebook comments from your WordPress site. Another plug-in, **Facebook comments SEO,** will insert a Facebook comment form, Open Graph tags, and insert all Facebook comments into your WordPress database for better search engine optimization. When it comes to spammers, Facebook with Open Graph is managing to weed out spammers and trolls with great effectiveness. Facebook allows you to login with Facebook, Yahoo, and Microsoft Live.
- **Disqus comment system:** The other popular comment system Disqus replaces your WordPress comment system with

comments hosted and powered by Disqus. It features threaded comments and replies, notifications and replies by email, aggregated comments and social mentions, full spam filtering, and black-and-white lists. Disqus allows you to login with Facebook, Twitter, and Google.

- **Facebook Chat:** This is great if you want to chat with your visitors in real time. When installed, Facebook Chat will display on the bottom right. This is great for supplying support on your site.

- **Broken Link Checker:** This essential plug-in scans your site and notifies you if it finds any broken links or missing images and then lets you replace the link with one that works.

- **RB Internal Links:** This plug-in assists you with internal links and cuts the risk of error pages and broken links.

- **Social Sharing Plugins:** There are numerous social sharing plugins available for WordPress. **Flare** is a simple yet eye-catching sharing bar that you can customize depending on which buttons you want to display. It helps to get you followed or 'liked' and helps get your content shared via posts, pages, and media types. The other great feature Flare has is that you can display your Flare at the top, bottom, or right of your post content. When Flare is displayed on the left and right of your posts, it follows your visitors down the page and conveniently hides when not needed. Other social sharing plug-ins include: **Floating Social Media Icon**, **Social Stickers,** and **Shareaholic,** to name but a few.

- **All-In-One Schema Rich Snippets:** Rich snippets are markup tags that webmasters can put in their sites in order to tell Google what type of content they have on their site so that Google can better display it in search results. It is basically a short summary of your page. Rich snippets are very interactive, let you stand out from your competition, and help with your search engine ranking. Unless you are a techie then implementing them can be tricky. However, this plug-in makes it really simple by giving you a meta box to fill in every time you create a new blog post.

- **Contact Form Plug-ins:** It is very important to make it easy for your visitors to contact you, and a form really does help with this. There are numerous plug-ins available for you to easily install, and here are a few: **Contact 7, Fast Secure Contact form, Contact form, and Contactme.**

- **Simple Pull Quote:** The Simple Pull Quote WordPpress plug-in provides an easy way for you to insert and pull quotes into your blog posts. This is great for bringing attention to important pieces of information and adding interest to a post.

- **Backup Plug-ins:** Backing up your files and database is essential. It may be that your hosting service provides this, but there are very good plug-ins that do this: Vaultpress, BackWPup, Backup buddy, and Backup.

- **Related Posts Plug-ins:** Related post plug-ins help your visitors to stay on your site by analyzing the content on your site and pulling in similar articles from your site for them to read. One of the most popular ones is **nrelate related** content which is simple to install and activate. **WordPress related posts** is another one.

- **Search Everything Plug-in:** This plug-in increases the ability of the WordPress search, and you can configure it to search for anything you choose.

- **Google Analytics Plugin:** The Google Analytics plug-in allows you to easily integrate Google Analytics using Google Analytics tracking code.

- **Google XML Sitemaps:** It is essential that the search engines can index your site and this plug-in will generate a special XML sitemap.

- **SEO Friendly images:** This plug-in automatically adds alt and title attributes to all your images, which helps to improve traffic from search engines.

- **Akismet (Comments and Spam):** The more traffic you receive, the more likely it is for you to receive spam and fake comments. Akismet checks your comments against Akismet web services to see if they look like spam or not and then lets you review it under your comments admin screen.

- **Social Author Bio:** Social Author Bio automatically adds an author box along with Gravatar and social icons on posts.
- **Thank Me Later:** This great little plug-in automatically sends a thank you note by email to anyone who has commented on your blog. You can personalize your email and set up exactly when you want to send it, and you can set it up to only send it out once or as a chain of emails. This plug-in is great for engaging people who comment on your blog, and you could use it to encourage people to join your opt-in.

## MEASURING YOUR RESULTS

Measuring the success of your blog is crucial in order to steer your blog in the right direction so that your business can benefit from all the rewards a top blog can offer. Here are a number of ways you can measure your success:

### Google Analytics

You can easily measure the number of social media shares, number of leads, subscribers, and comments on your blog. For more detailed information on your blog performance, setting up a Google Analytics account is essential and will offer you a wealth of detailed information so you can measure results, including the following:

- **The number of back links:** In the left side bar under **Standard Reports** you will find a section **Traffic Sources,** and then under **Social,** you will find **Trackbacks**. You will find here any web pages that have linked to any page of your site with the number of visits.
- **The number of visits:** Obviously this is one of the most important statistics, and you will be able to easily see how many visits you have and information about where your traffic is coming from.
- **Page views:** You will be able to see which pages are generating

the most interest, and therefore, you will be able to plan more content similar to this.

- **Keywords:** You can keep track of your success with how your traffic is being generated by keywords. You will be able to see if your optimization for certain keywords are working and whether your blog is being found by keywords that you had not considered. When you identify which keywords are the most popular, you can try and work them into other blog posts.

- **Conversions:** In Google Analytics you will also be able to track conversions, which is an action on your site that is important to your business. This could be a download, sign up, or purchase. You will need to define your goals in analytics in order to track the conversion. You will be able to see conversion rates and also the value of conversions if you set a monetary value. There are detailed instructions available in Google Analytics on how to set this up, or you can employ a web developer or specialist to do it.

## CHAPTER FIFTEEN

### *THE ICING ON THE CAKE!*

FOLLOWING ALL THE steps, instructions, and strategies is going to go a long way to making your campaign succeed, but what does it take to make you really good? If you have ever followed or are following certain brands on social media, you will probably have discovered that there are certain brands or businesses that stand out from the crowd. These are the brands and businesses that seem bigger than their products. These are the ones who usually have a sizeable and highly targeted audience, the best quality content, the greatest amount of interaction and engagement, and often post viral content. They literally have their audience hanging on their every word and get the highest open rates for their emails. They appear to understand their audience and relate to them by going out of their way by either helping them to achieve their dreams, calm their fears or confirm their suspicions, and offer them incredible value. It is obvious by the interaction that they have built a loving and respecting community, and you can be almost sure that all this is transferring to their balance sheets. These businesses are what I call 'The Social Media Superstars.' They are the game changers and they truly know how to leverage the power of social media to work for their business.

These 'Social Media Superstars' can often be compared to those party animals who always seem to be the most popular at any party and are more often than not surrounded by an audience of engaged and happy people having a great time. These people also always seem to be the most interesting, the most interested, the most charismatic, and the most engaged. They almost always tend to be good listeners as well. So how can you emulate this scenario, and what does it take to stand out from the crowd in LinkedIn marketing?

## It's all about your audience and a few other things!

The reasons these individuals, businesses, and brands are good at social media marketing is not because they have particular powers. It's not by chance or coincidence. It's because they know that it's all about the audience and a few other things!

Of course your aim is to ultimately benefit your business, but in order to do this you need to make it all about your audience and what they want. If you give them what they want by either making their life better or easier in some way or solving a problem they may have, then you are going to build a valuable base of fans who trust you, open your emails, and are ready to go to the next step and buy your product. You will find that your fans will become ambassadors and advocates and will then be doing the work for you by sharing your content and promoting your brand in the most powerful way, word-of-mouth. To achieve this and stand out from the crowd, you need to go the extra mile by doing the following:

- Being fully committed and positive about your campaign and in it for the long term
- Totally believing in what you are offering. This could be your product, your service, or yourself, if you are a personal brand.
- Making it all about your audience, knowing exactly who they are, what makes them tick, what they need, and how to connect with them
- Putting your audience's needs above your own and demonstrating the rich content and service you provide
- Putting the relationship with your audience first, by listening to them, understanding them, and embracing conversation where you can
- Offering your audience incredible value with free information and advice
- Being authentic and true to your brand

So if there is one piece of insight I want to leave you with, it is this:

## IT'S ALL ABOUT YOUR AUDIENCE and WHAT THEY WANT

I really hope you have enjoyed the book, have found it of great value, and that you will continue using it as your manual for your success on LinkedIn. The world of social media is continually changing, and it is my commitment to keep updating the books when these changes happen. If you would like to continue receiving these social media updates by email, please sign up at www.alexstearn.com

I would love your feedback about the book and would be very grateful if you could take just a moment to leave a review on Amazon at this link . By leaving a review you can also enter the Prize draw for a Kindle Fire HD at this link and of course please feel free to contact me if you have any questions at alex@alexstearn.com

I have also written a series covering all the major social media platforms including: Facebook, Google + , Pinterest, Instagram, Tumblr, YouTube and Twitter. The content on social media is common to all books and therefore if you are planning be purchase more I would suggest purchasing the big book which includes the complete series Make Social Media Work for your Business is available on Amazon from $9.99 available at this link http://bit.ly/alexauthor

Lastly, I have also set up a group on Facebook 'Make Social Media Work for your Business' The group was created for supporting each other in our social media efforts, for networking and also as a place to find out about the latest social media developments. You can join at this link http://bit.ly/yourgroup

I will also be continually posting helpful and inspirational tips on my LinkedIn account, and look forward to connecting with you there or on any of your preferred social networks.

Website: www.alexstearn.com
www.linkedin.com/in/alexstearn
www.facebook.com/alexandrastearn
www.instagram.com/alexstearn
www.twitter.com/alexstearncom
www.pinterest.com/alexstearn
www.alexstearn.tumblr.com
www.youtube.com/alexstearn
www.google.com/+alexstearn

# The complete series in one book!

If you liked this book and wish to purchase any of the other books in the series I would suggest the most cost effective way of doing this is to purchase the big book that includes all the titles rather than the individual titles.

Make Social Media Work for your Business is available from $9.99

## Make Social Media Work for your Business

The complete guide to marketing your business, generating new leads, finding new customers, and building your brand on Twitter, Pinterest, LinkedIn, Instagram, Google +, Tumblr, YouTube, Facebook, Foursquare,Vine and Snapchat.

## Individual Books

## Make Facebook Work for your Business

## Make Twitter Work for your Business

## Make Instagram Work for your Business

## Make Pinterest Work for your Business

## Make Google + Work for your Business

# <u>Make YouTube Work for your Business</u>

# <u>Make Tumblr Work for your Business</u>

# We'd love to hear from you

Thank you for your recent purchase of 'Make LinkedIn Work for your Business' I really hope you have enjoyed the book and your business will benefit greatly.

If you have any questions about the book or about social media marketing in general, please do not hesitate to contact me by email at **alex@alexstearn.com** or on **Facebook at www.facebook.com/alexandrastearn** and I will do my best to reply as soon as possible. I also offer regular updates, ebooks and social media tips in my newsletter at www.alexstearn.com and a group on Facebook which is all about supporting each other in our social media efforts and networking. Would love you to join us at this link
http://bit.ly/yourgroup

Lastly, if you have enjoyed the book I would also be so grateful if you could leave a review on Amazon, your feedback is so valuable and also helps others benefit from your experience.

Looking forward to seeing you in the group צ

16244931R00094

Printed in Great Britain
by Amazon